MAKE UP YOUR MIND

...ABOUT THE ISSUES OF LIFE

MAKE UP YOUR MIND

...ABOUT THE ISSUES OF LIFE

Charles R. Swindoll

MULTNOMAH PRESS
PORTLAND, OREGON 97266

OTHER BOOKS BY CHARLES R. SWINDOLL

For Those Who Hurt
Second Wind: A Fresh Run at Life
Killing Giants, Pulling Thorns
Home: Where Life Makes Up Its Mind
Strike the Original Match

You and Your Child
Hand Me Another Brick
Three Steps Forward, Two Steps Back

Improving Your Serve

BOOKLETS

Commitment	Tongues
Divorce	God's Will
Integrity	Demonism
Singleness	Sensuality

Unless otherwise identified, Scripture quotations are from the New American Standard Bible, copyright The Lockman Foundation 1960, 1961, 1962, 1963, 1968, 1971, 1972, 1973, 1975, 1977. Used by permission.

Scripture quotations marked TLB are from The Living Bible, copyright 1971 by Tyndale House Publishers, Wheaton, Illinois. Used by permission.

Scripture quotations marked Amplified Bible are from The Amplified New Testament, copyright 1954, 1958, by The Lockman Foundation. Used by permission.

Scripture quotations marked MLB are from The Modern Language Bible, The New Berkeley Version in Modern English, copyright 1945, 1959, 1969 by Zondervan Publishing House. Used by permission.

Scripture quotations marked RSV are from the Revised Standard Version of the Bible, copyright 1946, 1962, © 1971, 1973, Division of Christian Education, National Council of the Churches of Christ in the U.S.A. Used by permission.

Scripture quotations marked Good News Bible are from the Good News Bible: The Bible in Today's English Version, copyright 1976 by the American Bible Society. Used by permission.

PHOTOGRAPHY CREDITS: GARY BRAASCH (cover, pages 37, 61), DAVID CAVAGNARO (pages 19, 25, 45, 77, 81), DEWITT JONES (pages 29, 49, 57, 69), RUSS LAMB (page 11), BRUCE J. RUSSELL (page 89).

DESIGN BY: DANNELLE PFEIFFER

MAKE UP YOUR MIND
© 1981 by Multnomah Press
Printed in the United States of America

Library of Congress Cataloging in Publication Data

Swindoll, Charles R.
    Make up your mind.

    1. Decision (Christian theology)   2. Decisionmaking (Ethics)
I. Title.
BT02.S95   248.4   81-3978
ISBN 0-930014-61-8 (pbk.)   AACR2

CONTENTS

A WORLD COLORED GRAY

Color our world gray.

Not dogmatic black or absolute white. Not crystal clear, but foggy. Uncertain. Opaque rather than obvious. Cloudy. You know, really unsettled and unsure . . . loose, in neutral.

"Open-minded" is the chic way to express it. Stay away from whatever and whoever smacks of firm convictions and final conclusions. Emphasize feelings and process, but come down hard on answers that button down the issues.

Ours is a day of vague dialogue rather than strong declaration. Doctrine is viewed with a jaundiced eye in our generation of discussion, rethinking, talk shows, and rap sessions. It is now uncool to come to grips with no-other-option decisions, to work through the pros and cons with a view to saying yes or no. Anytime you want to take a vote, the grays have it by a wide margin.

Actually, this is not a new disease. It's been around for decades. But now it is coming out of the closet. Boldly. Without much hesitation. Clothed in the garb of humility, it catches us off guard . . . as G. K. Chesterton (the nineteenth-century C. S. Lewis) once put it:

What we suffer from today is humility in the wrong place. Modesty has moved from the organ of ambition to the organ of conviction, where it was never meant to be. A man was meant to be doubtful about himself, but undoubting about the truth; this has been exactly reversed. We are on the road to producing a race of men too mentally modest to believe in the multiplication table![1]

Mental modesty. Reluctance to accept, embrace, rely on, and openly declare ourselves. Even on the most obvious, the most basic of subjects.

This has been bothering me for several years. Not that I'm against discussion or differing opinions—whoever knows me well knows better than that—but that so much *stays* up in the air. So many things *remain* unsure even though the Bible tells it straight, leaving us with no other alternative than getting off the fence of indecision. More often than not God is saying, "Make up your mind!" rather than, "Let's hear another opinion."

This is a book that asks you to do that very thing. It is designed to make you think . . . to realize what is at stake if you buy the gray, indecisive, ever-shifting, never-settling message of our times. It is a book that agrees with Paul's commentary on "the last days" as being days in which people are

> *. . . led on by various impulses, always learning and never able to come to the knowledge of the truth* (2 Timothy 3:6b-7).

I am indebted to John Sloan, the splendid editor of Multnomah Press, as well as the publisher, John Van Diest, for their insightful and penetrating counsel. And to Helen Peters for her diligence, skill, and keen eye as she typed and retyped this manuscript with such constant attention to detail. Of course, I am grateful to my family for their unselfish understanding as I was forced to "set my face like a flint" to get this project completed.

If our Lord uses these words to move you from the endless, futile syndrome of always discussing and never making up your mind, the effort involved in getting this book into print will have been worth it all.

If that occurs in your life, color me pleased.

Charles R. Swindoll

This book is affectionately dedicated
to my sister
LUCI SWINDOLL
my decisive, efficient, delightful friend
whose contagious humor and
constant support have
encouraged my life beyond measure.

...ABOUT TRUTH AND ERROR

Truth. Error.

Those terms seem so clear on a sheet of paper. **Truth:** that which is reliable, objective, worth our confidence, deserving of our trust, foundational. **Error:** that which is wrong, something we need to shun, reject, deny. Stuff that we have no business getting involved in.

But all that clarity seems fuzzy when we wrap those two absolutes in the garb of human circumstances. And then add the impressive appeal of majority opinion, theoretical questions, ethical situations, and emotional attractions. All that objectivity fades.

Truth seems strangely shaded. Occasionally even rigid. And our feelings do a number on us. They twist truth into a role of something between unfair and intolerant. Enter error. That chameleon actor who loves to take up the slack. And instead of appearing with fangs, black beady eyes, and a hiss, it smiles warmly and graciously asks questions:

"Has God said . . . ?"

And even makes promises like, "If you yield, you'll be like God."

Let's come to terms with truth.

Let's stop embracing error.

Let's decide now. Such is the counsel of James Russel Lowell:

> "Once to every man and nation
> comes the moment to decide,
> In the strife of Truth with Falsehood,
> for the Good or evil side."[2]

Maybe some of these things will help you make up your mind about truth and error.

Think with Discernment

There is a Persian proverb that sounds more like a tongue twister than sound advice. My high school speech teacher had us memorize it for obvious reasons:

He who knows not, and knows not that he knows not, is a fool; shun him.

He who knows not, and knows that he knows not, is a child; teach him.

He who knows, and knows not that he knows, is asleep; wake him.

He who knows, and knows that he knows, is wise; follow him.

All four "types" can be found on every campus, in any business, among all neighborhoods, within each church. They don't wear badges nor do they introduce themselves accordingly. You'll never have someone walk up, shake your hand, and say, "Hi, I'm Donald. I'm a fool." Chances are good that the *last* thing he will want you to discover is the deep-down truth that "he knows not, and knows not that he knows not."

Then how in the world are we to know whom to shun, to teach, to awaken, or to follow? *Discernment* is the answer. Skill and accuracy in reading character. The ability to detect and identify the real truth. To see beneath the surface and correctly "size up" the situation. To read between the lines of the visible.

Is it a valuable trait? Answer for yourself. When God told Solomon to make a wish—any wish—and it would be granted, the king responded:

". . . give Thy servant an understanding heart to judge Thy people to discern between good and evil" (1 Kings 3:9).

And who doesn't know about the wisdom of Solomon to this very day? Paul informs us that discernment is one characteristic that accompanies genuine spirituality (1 Corinthians 2:14-16). Hebrews 5:14 calls it a mark of maturity. Discernment, you see, gives one a proper frame of reference, a definite line separating good and evil. It acts as an umpire in life and blows the whistle on the spurious. It's as particular as a pathologist peering into a microscope. Discernment picks and chooses its dates with great care. It doesn't fall for fakes

. . . or flirt with phonies
. . . or dance with deceivers
. . . or kiss counterfeits goodnight.

Come to think of it, discernment would rather relax alone at night with the Good Book than mess around with the gullible gang. You see, it's from that Book that discernment learns to distinguish the fools from the children . . . and the sleeping from the wise.

Before you start in on the old bromide, "But that doesn't sound very loving!" better take another look at John's counsel. You remember John. He's the guy known for his tender love for Jesus. He wrote:

> Beloved, do not put faith in every spirit, but prove (test) the spirits to discover whether they proceed from God . . .
> (1 John 4:1, Amplified Bible).

In today's talk—"Stop believing everything you hear. Quit being so easily convinced. Be selective. Think. Discern!"—undiscerning love spawns and invites more heresy than any of us are ready to believe. One of the tactics of survival when facing "the flaming missiles of the evil one" (Ephesians 6:16) is to make certain we have cinched up the belt of *truth* rather tightly around ourselves. And what helps us do battle with the enemy also strengthens us in relationships with friends.

A Christian without discernment is like a submarine in a harbor plowing full speed ahead without radar or a periscope. Or a loaded 747 trying to land in dense fog without instruments or a radio. Lots of noise, a great deal of power, good intentions . . . until. I don't have another Persian proverb to describe the outcome, but who needs it? It happens day in, day out . . . with disastrous regularity.

Do I hear you say you want it, but don't know where to go to find it?

- Go to your *knees.* James 1:5 promises wisdom to those who ask for it.
- Go to the *Word.* Psalm 119:98-100 offers insight beyond our fondest dreams.
- Go to the *wise.* Discernment is better caught than taught. Those who have the disease are often highly contagious.

This offer is good throughout life and comes with a satisfaction-guaranteed clause. All may apply, even those who think they know it all, and know not that they know nothing.

Watch Out for Fakes

A friend of mine ate dog food one evening. No, he wasn't at a fraternity initiation or a hobo party . . . he was actually at an elegant student reception in a physician's home near Miami. The dog food was served on delicate little crackers with a wedge of imported cheese, bacon chips, an olive, and a sliver of pimento on top. That's right, friends and neighbors, it was hors d'oeuvres *a la Alpo*.

The hostess is a first-class nut! You gotta know her to appreciate the story. She had just graduated from a gourmet cooking course, and so she decided it was time to put her skill to the ultimate test. Did she ever! After doctoring up those miserable morsels and putting them on a couple of silver trays, with a sly grin she watched them disappear. One guy (my friend) couldn't get enough. He kept coming back for more. I don't recall how they broke the news to him . . . but when he found out the truth, he probably barked and bit her on the leg! He certainly must have gagged a little.

Ever since hearing that story—it is actually the truth—I've thought about how perfectly it illustrates something that transpires *daily* in another realm. I'm referring to religious fakes . . . professional charlatans . . . frauds . . . counterfeit Christians who market their wares on shiny platters decorated with tasty persuasion and impressive appearance. Being masters of deceit, they serve up delectable dishes camouflaged by logical-sounding phrases.

Hey, that's smart! If you want to make a counterfeit dollar bill, you don't use yellow construction paper, cut it in the shape of a triangle, put the Lone Ranger's picture in the center, and stamp "3" on each corner. That deceives nobody. Deception comes in *convincing* fashion, wearing the garb of authenticity, supported by the credentials of intelligence, popularity, and even a touch of class. By the millions, gullible gluttons are duped into swallowing lies, thinking all the while they are digesting the truth. In reality they are underscoring the well-worn words of Phineas Taylor Barnum: *"There's a sucker born every minute."*

> *For such men are false apostles, deceitful workers, disguising themselves as apostles of Christ. And no wonder, for even Satan disguises himself as an angel of light. Therefore it is not surprising if his servants also disguise themselves as servants of righteousness . . .* (2 Corinthians 11:13-15).

A glance at the silver platter and everything looks delicious: "apostles of Christ . . . angels of light . . . servants of righteousness." Through the genius of disguise, they not only look good, they *feel* good, they *smell* good! The media serves them under your nose.

Testimonies abound! Listen to some:

"This is new . . . it has changed my life!"

Others say, "I did what he said . . . and now God speaks to me directly. I see visions. I can *feel* God."

Over two million freely shout, "Eternity is *now* . . . materialism is godly. Getting rich is a sign of spirituality."

A larger band of followers claim, "We own nothing. Everything goes to the guru."

You find them everywhere. On street corners with little magazines, looking ever so dedicated to God. Staring up at the stars, discovering the future. Sitting in small groups on hillsides, eating canary mix, refusing to shave or bathe lest they interrupt their "communion with God." The platter is filled with variety! You find some attending religious pep rallies led by flamboyant cheerleaders in $800 orange suits and diamond-studded shoes. On the opposite extreme are mysti-cal dreamers who prefer seclusion as they squat in silence.

They may have a "new" look, feel and taste like the real thing—but they are not. As Screwtape once quoted to Wormwood their father's couplet:

Old error in new dress
is ever error nonetheless.[3]

which is another way of saying, "Dog food is dog food, no matter how you decorate it." Or, as Paul put it so pointedly, "They are false . . . deceitful . . . disguising themselves as apostles of Christ." They may not look like it, but they are as phony as a yellow $3 bill.

Unfortunately, as long as there are hands to pick from the platter, there will be good-looking, sweet-smelling tidbits available. But some day, some dreadful day, the final Judge will determine and declare truth from error. There will be a lot of gagging and choking . . . and it will no longer taste good.

Nothing tastes good in hell.

Stay on Target

It was one of those days.

People. Demands. Deadlines. Big decisions. Frustration over not reaching desired goals. Endless interruptions mixed with a nagging headache that *Excedrin* wouldn't erase and positive thinking wouldn't help. You know, one of those door-slamming, what's-the-use? days that comes about once a week, lasts into the evening . . . and will spend the night with you if you let it.

Right in the middle of the mess, a guy poked his head in the doorway, smiled, and (among other things) dropped a real gem on me. Preoccupied as I was, the impact of what he said didn't hit me until I was stacking up the stuff I needed to haul home and work on that night. I stopped stacking, cocked my head to the left, and thought deeply about his comment.

The person who knows **how** *will always have a job . . . and he will always work for the person who knows* **why.**

Good thought, huh?

Stop your fretting and stacking today long enough to drink that in. It will help you. It will force you, of course, to ask yourself, "In which camp am I?" Not that either is right or wrong. Just revealing. Now don't misunderstand, both are absolutely essential in our society. If you question that, try to picture a thousand Cherokee chiefs thundering into battle . . . or 216 presidents in the outfit you work for . . . or a shop full of auto mechanics where everybody dispatches jobs and writes paychecks . . . or a college with no faculty and a conference room stuffed full of deans . . . or 25 managers in the dug-out.

People who *know how* are on the front lines and in the trenches, selling the product, teaching the students, fixing the cars, typing the letters, swinging the bats, getting the job done. Those who are diligent and really know their stuff are invaluable. They will seldom have difficulty finding employment. One more fact: They will always be the largest in number among the working force.

But there must be those who *know why* in leadership. People who can harness the energy and give direction . . . people who can exercise management skills that result in motivation and enthusiasm among those who know how. The difficulty comes from three areas:

1. Those who *know why* spend too much time doing things that ought to be done by those who know how.

2. Those who *know how* don't know the *why* behind what they are doing.

3. Those who should *know why* don't know (and don't care) why!

If organizational management isn't your bag, you're bored and almost asleep by now. But for the few still reading, think about the importance of having and communicating the right philosophy behind what you're trying to accomplish. The further up you go in the organizational structure, the more the question "why" must be addressed.

That's absolutely essential in a local church, for example. Without it we systematically engage in putting out daily fires, try to wear too many hats, wonder what our priorities are, and fight furiously with the most vicious beast on earth—*guilt.*

Jesus Christ—our ultimate Leader—has clearly declared our philosophy:

> *And He gave some as apostles, and some as prophets, and some as evangelists, and some as pastors and teachers, for the equipping of the saints for the work of service, to the building up of the body of Christ* (Ephesians 4:11-12).

Don't just scan those words; study them. They form the target of the local church—but they have been virtually ignored in this day of maddening activity. If we move very far from this target, we miss the mark.

• Why has the Lord given leadership? To equip saints.

• Why are saints to be equipped? To serve.

• Why is it so important to serve? To build up the body.

These are not multiple choice questions—not pick-and-choose issues. They are our foundation . . . our bottom-line philosophy. Press these matters to the maximum and it's amazing how simple (and exciting!) our job really is. Who is the major target of our ministry? The Christian. What is the major need in his or her life? Being equipped to serve. Equipped through worship, instruction, and fellowship. Equipped to express himself in evangelism and missions . . . in the home, in the community, in the world. Everything we do, everything we promote and finance and endorse should relate directly to equipping and/or serving. That's the truth!

It's invaluable that people in the church know why and how. If we stay on target, there will be no reason for us to become fire fighters and beast slayers . . . or door slammers, for that matter.

Guard Your Integrity

With big boulders rumbling across life's landscape—like hostages in Iran, the talk of returning to the military draft, double-digit inflation, a European summit conference, and complex nuclear issues of various types—who's concerned about a distant, almost-forgotten pebble of the past? Like *Watergate*. Haven't we beaten that drum enough? I mean, names like Segretti and Liddy and Dean and Mitchell and Magruder and Ehrlichman and Haldeman and Kalmbach and Kleindiendst are now political relics of yesteryear. The whole sick scene has been put to bed, hasn't it? Along with the U-2, the Bay of Pigs, the Gulf of Tonkin incident, and Chappaquiddick, shouldn't we be realistic enough to admit that Watergate happened, wrong occurred, consequences followed, and we'll never know all the story?

Yes, I suppose. Far be it from me to go snooping around for a few harmless skeleton bones . . . if indeed they are harmless. But if there's another lesson to be learned from that national embarrassment, maybe it's worth the effort of exhuming and examining the remains yet again.

Part of my reason for doing so is prompted by a nagging desire to learn everything possible from previous blunders. In that sense, history along is a wise pedagogue. But another reason I'm intrigued is brought about by a book I've almost finished reading written by Leo Rangell, M.D., a psychiatrist who explores what he calls "the compromise of integrity" in his careful, articulate analysis of the inner workings within the head and psyche of Richard M. Nixon and several of his closest confidants. It's appropriately called *The Mind of Watergate*. Within the book is the transcript of a verbal investigation between Senator Baker and young Herbert L. Porter. Because the question-and-answer dialogue sets forth a basic issue worth pursuing, I'll repeat a segment of the account exactly as it transpired.

Baker: Did you ever have any qualms about what you were doing? . . . I am probing into your state of mind, Mr. Porter.

Porter: [Uncomfortably] I was not the one to stand up in a meeting and say that this should be stopped . . . I mean . . . I kind of drifted along.

The questioning continued.

Q: At any time did you ever think of saying, "I do not think this is quite right, this is not quite the way it ought to be." Did you ever think of that?

A: Yes, I did.

Q: What did you do about it?

A: I did not do anything.

Q: Why didn't you?

A: [After evidence of much inner thought on his face] In all honesty, probably because of the fear of group pressure that would ensue, of not being a team player.[4]

Porter's answer keeps coming back to haunt us these days. How much of that whole, ugly nightmare between the break-in in June of 1972 to the resignation of the President over two years later would have never happened if there had been the courage to stand alone?

What if, for example, the fear of doing wrong had been *greater* than "the fear of group pressure"? Or—the refusal to compromise one's personal integrity had been *stronger* than the desire to be loyal to the man at the top? This quality —peer courage—has to do with the retention of the capacity to think and to act as a separate individual while under the influence of the surrounding group.

Easy to say, but hard to do? Certainly! It's one thing to write stuff like this six, seven, eight years later after the fog has cleared and anybody can see the black-and-white issues. Hindsight always has 20-20. Monday morning quarterbacks and armchair generals have the same two things in common: clear perspective and correct decisions. But given the same pressures, fears, insecurities, uncertainties, and group intimidation at the time everything is caving in, it's terribly hard to stand pat and buck the tide. Few are the Joshuas who will stand up and say, "As for me and my house. . . ." Especially when nobody else is saying it. Or even thinking it.

All this strikes much closer to home than a break-in in D.C. or a breakdown in the Oval Office. It's a major motivation behind experimentation with drugs or sexual promiscuity or wholesale commitment to some cult or cooperation with an illegal financial scheme. Group pressure is terribly threatening. The screams and shouts of the majority have a way of intimidating integrity.

If it can happen among the upper crust of a nation, it should surprise no one that it can happen with ordinary folks like you and me. Be on guard! When push comes to shove, think independently. Think biblically. Do everything possible to lead with your head more than your feelings. If you fail to do this, you'll lose your ethical compass somewhere between your longing to be liked and your desire to do what is right. "Do not be misled," warns the apostle who often stood alone, "bad company corrupts good character" (1 Corinthians 15:33, NIV).

Watergate is well over eight years old. But a timeless lesson lingers: It is not so hard to know what is right to do as to do what you know is right. If being a "team player" requires doing what is wrong, you're on the wrong team.

God, Give Us Models

An usher met me as I was leaving the church several Sundays ago. He had been involved in counting the morning offering. He smiled as he walked up to me, stuck out his hand, and said, "I've got something for you. It came in the offering."

Here was a little hand-scribbled note from a child who had been in our worship service. It read:

TO PASTER CHUCK SWINDOL

I don't think you know me, but I shure know you. You are a very good speaker for Jesus Christ, I think your neet.

I even understand what you are saying and that's how it should be.

I LOVE YOU!

Guess what was attached to the note. A chocolate sucker, all wrapped in cellophane ready to be enjoyed.

Now, friend, that's admiration. When a darling little kid will surrender his prized possession . . . wow! This sucker means more to me than most any honor I could ever receive, because it represents something no amount of money can buy. A child's respect. Personal admiration. To some busy, active youngster tucked away in our vast congregation, I represent somebody he or she looks up to. And believes in.

I'm honest, it chokes me up. It also keeps me on my toes. Somewhere out there is a child whose eyes are on me . . . whose ears are tuned in . . . who's also pretty choosy. After all, it's wrapped in cellophane, tied with ribbon . . . and it hasn't even been licked (so far as I can tell).

Admiration. There's not much of it today. Maybe that explains the inordinate hunger for fantasy heroes like Batman, Superman, Luke Skywalker, and Rocky. There has never been a day when the athletic prima donnas have had larger fan clubs or weird musical groups bigger crowds. There was a time when patriotism provided us with all the models we needed. Remember? Why, who ever had the audacity to suggest a hint of suspicion against MacArthur . . . or "Ike" . . . or the local police department or the *FBI*, for that matter? The cop on the corner may have been stared at, but it was out of respect, not rebellion. Physicians were also admired. So were teachers. And lawyers. And preachers. And hard workers. And mothers.

What's happened? Why the low regard for leaders? Especially the outspoken ones who stand for decency and integrity and love for country, the flag, human dignity, and a wholesome respect for the family.

Has Watergate raped everyone's trust in anyone? Are all the police officers suspect? Must every preacher prove he's not an Elmer Gantry? Is it necessary for every surgeon to conduct his profession more concerned about a malpractice lawsuit than the gall bladder operation? Is corruption now so prevalent in government that young men and women with integrity no longer consider political science a viable major? Has the Viet Nam thing soured everybody against the military? I mean, where are the heroes?

Hymn-writer Isaac Watts' question should be changed from, "Are there no foes for me to face?" to, "Are there no models for me to follow?" And it would be a right-on query. Foes to face we have. Models to admire, we don't. At least it seems that way. Now we are like the best-sellers—*Looking Out for #1* and *Pulling Your Own Strings.*

Funny thing, when you write stuff like this, you feel a little dated . . . somewhat soap boxish. You sense there's a whole gang of quasi-sophisticates thinking, "There's the old *Marine* coming out in Swindoll again. Shades of Guadalcanal gung-ho . . . Americanism on parade." Well, if a confession will help, I openly admit I still get a chill down my spine when they play our national anthem at the Olympics. I also confess getting a little misty when I recall standing at ramrod attention saying the pledge of allegiance as a barefoot fourth-grader in Southmayd Elementary . . . then praying for a crippled president I had never seen, but admired more than words could say.

Our cynical, self-centered society would do well to restore an invaluable antique that has been cast aside, forgotten like a dust-covered treasure: admiration. As that restoration occurs, so will the *esprit de corps* of our nation, the morale that once gave us pride to pull together and passion to stand alone. Our children need it. So do our youth, as well as adults. Individuals we hold in high esteem, in whom the qualities of greatness are incarnated. People who mirror the bedrock principles of solid Christian character. Those things can neither be purchased nor inherited. Slowly, almost unawares, admiration becomes the carbon paper that transfers character qualities by the rubbing of one life against another.

Like Christ with His guys. Like a godly coach with the team. Like an authentic Christian businessman with his peers. Like a faithful dad with his family. Usually the model doesn't even consider himself such until something little happens.

Something as little as a chocolate sucker in the church offering plate on Sunday morning.

Digging for Silver

"Can you see anything?"

What a question to ask! Howard Carter's mouth and eyes were wide open when his aide asked it. His head was stuck into a timeless tomb. Beads of perspiration popped out on the British archaeologist's brow. For six straight years he had been digging. Endless trenches. Tons of rubble. Huge chunks of worthless debris. Nothing!

It was 1922. For more than a score of centuries, archaeologists, tourists, and tomb robbers had searched for the burial places of Egypt's pharaohs. It was believed that nothing remained undisturbed. Especially in the *Royal Valley* where the ancient monarchs had been buried for over half a millennium. Because nobody felt there was anything left to be discovered, Carter carried on his pursuit, privately financed, with only a few scraps of evidence to keep him going. Somewhere . . . somehow . . . he was convinced there was one remaining tomb. Twice during his six-year search he was within two yards of the first stone step leading to the burial chamber.

Finally—EUREKA!

Can you see anything?

That was like Pilot Michael Collins on July 20, 1969, asking Armstrong and Aldrin, "Do you feel anything?" as moon dust formed puffy white clouds around their boots.

Peering into silent darkness, Howard Carter saw what no modern man had ever seen. Wooden animals, statues, chests, gilded chariots, carved cobras, unguent boxes, vases, daggers, jewels, a throne, the wooden figure of the goddess Selket . . . and a hand-carved coffin of a teenaged king. In his own words, he saw "strange animals, statues, and gods—everywhere the glint of gold." It was, of course, the priceless tomb and treasure of King Tutankhamen, the world's most exciting archaeological discovery. More than 3000 objects in all, taking Carter about ten years to remove, catalog, and restore. "Exquisite!" "Incredible!" "Elegant!" "Magnificent!" "Ahhh!" must have passed his lips dozens of times when he first whispered his way through that ancient Egyptian cocoon.

There are few joys like the joy of sudden discovery. Instantly, there is forgotten the pain and expense of the search, the inconveniences, the hours, the sacrifices. Bathed in the ecstasy of discovery, time stands still. Nothing else seems half so important. Lost in the thrill of the moment, we relish the inexpressible finding—like a little child watching a worm.

Such discoveries have many faces . . .

- the answer to a lengthy conflict
- insight into your own makeup
- understanding the "why" behind a fear
- just the right expression to describe a feeling
- the reason your stomach churns in certain situations
- getting to know your child's "bent"
- a technique that saves time and energy
- a simple way to communicate something complicated
- motivating those who work under your direction
- finding relief from needless guilt

Solomon talks about the greatest discovery of all. He puts it in words that describe the activity of a guy like Howard Carter—except in this case, he isn't searching for King Tut. Listen:

"My son, if you will receive my sayings,
And treasure my commandments within you,
Make your ear attentive to wisdom,
Incline your heart to understanding;
For if you cry for discernment,
Lift your voice for understanding;
If you seek her as silver,
And search for her as for hidden treasures;
Then you will discern the fear of the LORD,
And discover the knowledge of God (Proverbs 2:1-5).

Talk about a discovery! Hidden in the Scriptures are priceless verbal vaults. Silent. Hard to find. Easy to miss if you're in a hurry. But they are there, awaiting discovery. God's Word, like a deep, deep mine, stands ready to yield its treasures.

Can you see anything?

Declaring Excuses

No offense, but some of you don't have any business reading this today. Normally, I do not restrict my words to any special group of people. But now I must. This time it is *for Christians only.* Everything I write from now to the end of this article on excuses is strictly for the believer in Christ. If you're not there yet, you can toss this aside because you lack a major ingredient: the power of God. Non-Christians are simply unable to choose righteous paths consistently. That divine response upon which the Christian can (and *must*) draw is not at the unbeliever's disposal. That is, not until personal faith in Jesus Christ is expressed. This is one of those now-not-later issues that's limited to believers only.

Now then, if you know the Lord, you are the recipient of limitless ability . . . incredible strength. Just read a few familiar lines out of the Book, *slowly* for a change:

> *I can do all things through Him who strengthens me* (Philippians 4:13).

> . . . *"My grace is sufficient for you, for power is perfected in weakness." Most gladly, therefore, I will rather boast about my weaknesses, that the power of Christ may dwell in me* (2 Corinthians 12:9).

> *For this reason, I bow my knees before the Father, . . .*

> *that He would grant you, according to the riches of His glory, to be strengthened with power through His Spirit in the inner man* (Ephesians 3:14, 16).

> . . . *He has granted to us His precious and magnificent promises, in order that by them you might become partakers of the divine nature . . .* (2 Peter 1:4).

And one more:

> *No temptation has overtaken you but such as is common to man; and God is faithful, who will not allow you to be tempted beyond what you are able, but with the temptation will provide the way of escape also, that you may be able to endure it* (1 Corinthians 10:13).

Wait a minute now. Did you read every word—or did you skip a line or two? If so, please go back and *slowly* graze over those five statements written to you, a Christian. It's really important.

Okay, what thought stands out the most? Well, if someone asked me that question, I'd say, "Special strength or an unusual ability from God." In these verses it's called several things: strength, power, divine nature, ability. God has somehow placed into the Christian's insides a special something, that extra inner reservoir of power that is more than a match for the stuff life throws at us. When in operation, phenomenal accomplishments are achieved, sometimes even *miraculous.*

Let's get specific.

It boils down to the choice of two common words in our vocabulary. Little words, but, oh, so different! "Can't" and "won't." Christians need to be very careful which one they choose. It seems that we prefer to use "can't."

"I just *can't* get along with my wife."

"My husband and I *can't* communicate."

"I *can't* discipline the kids like I should."

"I just *can't* give up the affair I'm having."

"I *can't* stop overeating."

"I *can't* find the time to pray."

"I *can't* quit gossiping."

No, any Christian who really takes those five passages we just looked at (there are dozens more) will have to confess the word really should be "won't." Why? Because we have been given the power, the ability to overcome. Literally! And therein lies hope in hoisting anchors that would otherwise hold us in the muck and mire of blame and self-pity.

One of the best books you can read this year on overcoming depression is a splendid work by two physicians, Minirth and Meier, appropriately entitled *Happiness Is a Choice.* These men agree:

> As psychiatrists we cringe whenever [Christian] patients use the word *can't.* . . .
> Any good psychiatrist knows that "I can't" and "I've tried" are merely lame excuses. We insist that our patients be honest with themselves and use language that expresses the reality of the situation. So we have our patients change their *can'ts* to *won'ts.* . . .
>
> If an individual changes all his *can'ts* to *won'ts,* he stops avoiding the truth, quits deceiving himself, and starts living in reality—. . . .[9]

"I just *won't* get along with my wife."

"My husband and I *won't* communicate."

"I *won't* discipline the kids like I should."

"I just *won't* give up the affair I'm having."

"I *won't* stop overeating."

"I *won't* find the time to pray."

"I *won't* quit gossiping."

Non-Christians have every right and reason to use "can't," because they really can't! They are victims, trapped and bound like slaves in a fierce and endless struggle. Without Christ and His power, they lack what it takes to change permanently. They don't because they can't! It is a fact . . . a valid excuse.

But people like us? Hey, let's face it, we don't because we won't . . . we disobey because we want to, not because we have to . . . because we choose to, not because we're forced to. The sooner we are willing to own up realistically to our responsibility and stop playing the blame game at pity parties for ourselves, the more we'll learn and change and the less we'll burn and blame.

Wish I could find a less offensive way to communicate all this, but I just can't.

Oops!

Holding Things Loosely

In her fine book, *Splinters in My Pride*, Marilee Zdenek reflects our deepest feelings. Those misty ones, hard to get a handle on. As the sights, sounds, and smells of different seasons began to create nostalgic itches inside me recently, she scratched one:

It was hard to let you go:
To watch womanhood reach out and snatch you
Long before the mothering was done.
But if God listened to mothers and gave in,
Would the time for turning loose of daughters
  ever come?

It was hard when you went away—
For how was I to know
The serendipity of letting go
Would be seeing you come home again
And meeting in a new way
Woman to woman—
Friend to friend.[7]

Letting go.

Turning loose.

Releasing the squeeze.

Being better at smothering than loving, we are blown away with the thought of relaxing our gargantuan grip. Because releasing introduces the terror of risk, the panic of losing control. The parting cannot happen without inward bleeding. The coward heart fears to surrender its prized toys. Even though it must say goodbye eventually.

Like losing a mate or a child. Experts tell us our first response is denial: "No!" In a rather extensive psychosomatic research project, the Holmes-Rahe Stress Test, I learned that most of us cannot cope with the full blast of 300 "life-change units" in any given 12-month period without the possibility of severe repercussions. Interestingly, among the stress experiences, losing a mate (100), losing a marriage (73), and losing a close family member (63) rated right at the top.[8] It's hard to let go. Turning loose heightens our stress.

Like releasing a dream; or allowing a child space to grow up; or letting a friend have the freedom to be and to do. What maturity that requires! What a test on our insecurity! The authoress is accurate:

. . . if God listened to mothers . . .
Would the time for turning loose . . . ever come?

Thank goodness, He doesn't.

We are often hindered from giving up our treasures out of

fear for their safety. But wait. Everything is safe which is committed to our God. In fact, nothing is really safe which is *not* so committed. No child. No job. No romance. No friend. No future. No dream.

Need some proof? Check out Abraham with his almost-adult son Isaac. Genesis 22. The old man's treasured delights rested in that boy. That relationship could well have bordered upon the perilous . . . if father would not come to grips with releasing son. But it was at that juncture that Jehovah-turned-pedagogue taught the patriarch a basic lesson in life.

> *"Take now your son, your only son, whom you love, Isaac, and go to the land of Moriah; and offer him there as a burnt offering . . ."* (Genesis 22:2).

It was time to turn him loose. Abraham might have started pleading or bargaining or manipulating, but that would not have caused the Almighty to choose an alternate course.

No—Abraham had to open his hands and surrender on that ancient altar the one thing that eclipsed the Son from his heart. It hurt cruelly . . . beyond imagination. But it was effective.

The greater the possessiveness, the greater the pain. The old miser within us will never lie down quietly and die obediently to our whisper. He must be torn out like a Cypress tap root. He must be extracted in agony and blood like a tooth from the jaw. And we will need to steel ourselves against his piteous begging, recognizing it as echoes from the hollow chamber of self-pity, one of the most hideous sins of the human heart.

What is it God wants me to do?

To hold all things loosely. That He might reign within without a rival. With no threats to His throne. And with just enough splinters in my pride to keep my hands empty and my heart warm.

Acting Decisively

*"Now then, revere the L*ORD*, and serve Him in sincerity and truth. Reject the gods which your ancestors served beyond the river and in Egypt, and serve the L*ORD*. However, if it seems wrong in your eyes to serve the L*ORD*, choose today whom you will serve—whether the gods whom your fathers served beyond the river or the gods of the Amorites in whose land you live. Nevertheless, I and my house, we shall serve the L*ORD*"* (Joshua 24:14-15, MLB).

I like Joshua's style. Like a good leader, he laid out the facts. He exhorted those about him to get off the fence and get their act together spiritually. He encouraged personal authenticity and strong commitment . . . but not once did he pull rank and fall back on intimidation to get his way. He risked being ignored and rejected when he left the final decision up to them. He respected their right to follow his advice or walk away when he told them, in so many words, "Make up your mind!" But there was never any question where he stood. He had weighed the evidence, considered the alternatives, and come to a settled conviction—he and his family were going to serve the Lord God, no question about it. But what *others* would do was strictly up to them. They would have to decide for themselves.

Unusual combination. A strong leader who knew where he was going, but gave others the space they needed to choose for themselves. No threats. No name-calling. No public putdowns. No exploitation or manipulation or humiliation. He didn't play on their emotions or attack their alleged ignorance or use some gimmick to gain strokes in defense of his position. He knew what God would have *him* do, and he realized the consequences of their choosing differently . . . but they needed to weigh those issues for themselves. It needed to be *their* decision, not his. At that point, he backed off and said, "Now *you* decide."

That's not only smart, it's an evidence of two admirable virtues: security in himself and respect for others. Today, it is clear to all of us that Joshua made the right decision back then. From our objective perspective, he chose the correct alternative . . . as they also did later on. But for him to hurry them to opt for *his* position, without their wrestling with the issues on their own, would result in a superficial and rather fragile decision that would later melt under the heat of difficulty.

Nevertheless, there will always be some who want others to make their decisions for them. Many individuals in Christendom are continually looking for some evangelical guru or superstar pastor or bionic authority figure to cosign for their lives. As David Gill was quoted saying in *Radix* magazine:

We want heroes! We want reassurance that someone knows what is going on in this mad world. We want a father or a mother to lean on. We want revolutionary folk heroes who will tell us what to do until the rapture. We massage the egos of these demagogues and canonize their every opinion.[10]

It takes the restraining power of the Holy Spirit to withstand such tempting invitations to take control. It is helpful to remember that every time we yield to that destructive desire for power we retard others' growth toward maturity. Making one's own decisions develops healthy mental muscles. But, I repeat, there will always be a few who crave to be told what to do. They are the ones who remain so indecisive their favorite color is plaid.

A major reason some prefer to be indecisive is laziness. Decision making is hard work. Peter Drucker is correct when he says:

A decision is a judgment. It is a choice between alternatives. It is rarely a choice between right and wrong. It is at best a choice between "almost right" and "probably wrong"—but much more often a choice between two courses of action, neither of which is provably more nearly right than the other.[11]

That may sound like a tongue-twister, but in reality it's a mind-boggler, requiring a painful, exacting process rare to many, called *thinking.*

How much easier it is to adopt a list, to click off the answers one, two, three, four, five. You don't have to think. All you need to do is follow instructions. Don't weigh the consequences. Don't sweat the details. Just do as you are told and leave the driving to "us," namely, a few guys at the top. Don't think it through and decide . . . just submit.

If that is the approach you prefer, let me remind you of two words, just two words—*Watergate* and *Jonestown.*

Decisiveness in both of those tragedies was replaced with blind obedience, unquestioned authority, and absolute loyalty. Somebody, somehow, at some time in each of those outfits convinced the troops that Tennyson's battle cry for the Light Brigade was the standard operating procedure for them:

Theirs not to make reply,
Theirs not to reason why, Theirs but to do and die.

There is a place for that philosophy in the military where there isn't time to stop and think. Rap sessions aren't too popular in combat when the objective is survival.

But in day-to-day living, when issues are not clearly spelled out in Scripture, when there is a lot of gray instead of black and white, we need to learn a lesson from Moses' mature successor.

Think wisely. Weigh the alternatives. Choose for yourself. *You* decide. Now.

Unplugging the TV Drug

A fascinating experiment on addiction was reported in a recent issue of *Good Housekeeping* magazine.[12] Not drug addiction. Not alcohol addiction. Not tobacco or candy addiction. It was on television addiction.

A Detroit newspaper made an offer to 120 families in the city. The families were promised $500 each if they would agree not to watch TV for one month. That's right—500 bucks if they'd keep the tube turned off for just 30 days. Guess how many turned down the offer.

Ninety-three.

Of the 27 families that said yes, 5 were studied and reported on in the magazine article. Right away you realize it was quite an adjustment for them. Each family had been watching television from 40 to 70 hours a week . . . that's between 5.7 and 10 hours *a day.* Think of it! Every day of every week the monotonous sounds and electronic pictures were a continual part of those households—year in and year out.

Serious pains accompanied the sudden, cold-turkey withdrawal from the plug-in drug. Remarkable things occurred, some almost bizarre. Like the lady who started talking to the cat or the couple who *stopped* talking to each other altogether!

But some good things also occurred. Books were pulled off the shelf, dusty from neglect, and read. Families played games, listened to the radio, and enjoyed playing records together. In another family two young kids spent some time practicing how to spell their names and addresses!

Miracle of miracles, several actually reported the younger kids took their baths at night without throwing a fit. And *some* (better sit down) willingly practiced their piano lessons.

The results? Well, the "no TV month" families finally had to admit four facts:

1. Their family members were brought closer together.
2. More eyeball-to-eyeball time between parents and children took place.
3. There was a marked increase in patience between family members.
4. Creativity was enhanced.

I would love to report otherwise . . . but I must be honest rather than wishful and add that television eventually won out once again. All five families returned to their addiction for nearly the same numbers of hours as before. Some *more.*

It's not the TV that disturbs me. No, all it is is another

gadget that can be used and enjoyed on occasion. It's the abuse that bothers me—the paralyzing addiction that stifles human creativity and cripples personal relationships. I agree with the comment made in the Christian Medical Society Journal a couple of years ago:

The primary danger of the television screen lies not so much in the behaviour it produces as the behaviour it prevents.[13]

Turning on the television set can turn off the process that transforms children into people . . . and nonplus viewers into thinking, caring persons. That's why the little 9-year-old kid in San Francisco was overheard saying:

"I'd lot rather watch TV than play outside 'cause it's boring outside. They always have the same rides, like swings and things."[14]

One reputable authority declares that children raised on television come to adulthood with no evident signs of decline in overall intelligence. There is apparently no huge brain drain, but there are a few peculiarities that concern the pros in this field.

• Increased communication in a near nonverbal speech ("like man . . . uh . . . you know . . . uh . . .")
• Much less spontaneity and fewer imaginative concepts coming from young adults

• An intense, almost irrational, dependence on music with a heavy beat as their only art form
• The ever-present drug scene
• Greater interest in passive experiences than those requiring mental interaction and active involvement.

Since television sets sit in 97 percent of American homes (more homes have TV than indoor plumbing), these problems aren't decreasing.

Hey, let's do something about this, folks! It's a tough, uphill battle, but it *isn't* insurmountable. Coming off the addiction is always hard. It actually boils down to the correct use of two of the smallest things in your house, the on-off knob on your set and the simple yet powerful word "No." Now, don't look around for much support. You'll have to hammer out your own philosophy. One that fits you and your family. But, for sure, do something soon. Let's take seriously these words:

Fix your thoughts on what is true and good and right. Think about things that are pure and lovely, and dwell on the fine, good things in others.
Paul, to 20th-century Christians
(Philippians 4:8, TLB)

Believe me, the ultimate benefits you'll enjoy will be worth much more than $500 and they will certainly last a lot longer.

For a change, unplug the plug-in drug.

Do it now. Not later.

Dealing with Disillusionment

The prophet was in the pits. Literally. Like Poe's fanciful character, he was "sick, sick unto death." Swamped with disillusionment and drowning in despair, he cursed the day he was born and wondered why an abortion wasn't performed, killing him prior to his birth.

He screamed:

> *Why did I ever come forth from the womb To look on trouble and sorrow, So that my days have been spent in shame?* (Jeremiah 20:18)

An exaggeration? Not hardly. Read the record for yourself. Jeremiah's journal holds nothing back. In Chapter 20 the chief officer in the temple had him beaten (40 lashes), then placed in stocks. That means his feet, hands, and neck were secured in a torturous device that caused the body to be bent almost double. That happened after he was beaten! Why? Had he committed some crime? No. He had simply declared the truth. He had done what was right—and this is what he got in return. It hurt him deeply.

On top of all that, sarcastic whisperings swirled about. His once-trusted friends tagged him with a nickname—MAGOR-MISSABIB—meaning "terror on every side." That also hurt.

He must have felt like a limp rag doll in the mouth of a snarling Doberman.

His prayers became laced with loneliness and bold complaints:

> *O LORD, Thou hast deceived me and I was deceived. Thou hast overcome me and prevailed. I have become a laughingstock all day long; Everyone mocks me. . . .for me the word of the LORD has resulted In reproach and derision all day long* (Jeremiah 20:7-8).

The man is in anguish. Prophet or not, he is struggling with God's justice, His strange treatment. Deep down he is questioning His presence. "Where is He? Why has Jehovah vanished at a time when I need Him the most?"

The ancient man of God is not alone with feelings like that. Who hasn't wrestled with similar questions and doubts? Few express it more vividly than Elie Wiesel in the terse, tightly packed sentences of his book, *Night.* Wiesel, a Jew, spent his teenaged years in a Nazi death camp at Birkenbau. His young eyes witnessed tragedies too horrible to repeat. The toll it took on him is best described in the foreword by French Nobel-prize-winning author Francois Mauriac:

For him (Wiesel), Nietzsche's cry expressed an almost physical reality: God is dead, the God of love, of gentleness, of comfort . . . has vanished forevermore. . . . And how many pious Jews have experienced this death. On that day, horrible even among those days of horror, when the child watched the hanging of another child, who, he tells us, had the face of a sad angel, he heard someone behind him groan: 'Where is God? Where is He? Where can He be now?'[15]

What desperate feelings!

And one need not be in a concentration camp to have those thoughts. Or doubled over in stocks and beaten with rods. No, sometimes they come in the long, dark tunnel of suffering when the pain won't go away. Or when a marriage partner who promised to stay "for better or for worse" breaks that vow. Or when a long, sought-after dream goes up in smoke. Or when we kiss a loved one goodbye for the last time.

Not always . . . but sometime (usually unuttered and hidden away in the secret vaults of our minds) we question Jehovah's justice. We ask, "Is He absent today?" Personally, I cannot bring myself to chide Jeremiah. The heavens above him appeared as brass. His Lord's passivity disillusioned him. The silence of God was more than he could take. There are such times, I openly confess, when I, too, wonder about why He permits certain things to occur that seemingly defy His character.

At those times I'm tempted to say what the prophet said:

"I will not remember Him Or speak anymore in His name . . ." (20:9a).

"That's it! I'm tossing in my collar. No more sermons and devotionals for this preacher. Secular job here I come!" But right about the time I start to jump, I experience what Jeremiah admitted:

". . . Then in my heart it becomes like a burning fire Shut up in my bones; And I am weary of holding it in, And I cannot endure it" (20:9b).

Directly sent from God is this strong surge of hope, this cleansing fire of confidence, this renewed sense of determination swelling up within me. And the disillusionment is quietly replaced with His reassurance as He reminds me of that glorious climax to the hymn I often sing back to Him in full volume:

"All is well, all is well!"

Thank God, it is. Recently, I doubted that—like Jeremiah. But not today. Reassurance has returned. Divine perspective has provided a fresh breeze of hope in the pits. I have determined that disillusionment must go. Now . . . not later.

Like old *Magor-Missabib*, I ain't about to quit! God has broken through the brass above. With antiphonal voice His angels answer, "All is well, all is well!"

Taking Time

Eight words are brashly smeared across the dashboard of the speedboat tied up at Gulf Shores, Alabama. They reflect the flash and flair of its owner whose fast life is often publicized in sporting news across America. In the off-season, the left-handed speedster in the Gulf of Mexico resembles a shiftless, beachcombing drifter with his stubble beard, disheveled hair, and darting eyes rather than one of the highest-paid quarterbacks in Oakland Raider history. If his profession doesn't fit his looks, his nickname certainly does. *SNAKE.* As swift and sneaky in a swamp as he is on the field, Ken Stabler knows one speed . . . full throttle.

So we shouldn't be surprised to read the saucy sign on his dashboard that warns all passengers:

GET IN, SIT DOWN, SHUT UP, HANG ON.

If you plan to ride with Snake Stabler, be ready for one sustained roar during the trip. Somehow there's this itch inside him that isn't scratched, apart from that scream of an engine and the blur of salt water waves rushing beneath to the tune of 80+ miles per hour. Once you get in and sit down, you have the distinct feeling that shutting up and hanging on comes naturally. Once you've committed yourself to such an accelerated velocity, nothing short of survival really matters.

All that's okay if survival is the only thing that matters. If, however, the things that make life rich and meaningful to us (and those traveling with us) involve more than survival, then speed is an awfully thin wire to hang from. In other words, if we really want some things to count, if we genuinely desire some depth to emerge, some impact to be made, some profound and enduring investment to cast a comforting shadow across another's life (your child, a friend, whomever), it is essential that we slow down . . . at times, stop completely. And think. Now . . . not later. Don't you dare put this off another day!

My oldest son and I were lingering in a local gift shop some time ago. Our eyes fell upon a row of large posters that were framed and stacked together. We laughed at some nutty ones, we studied some serious ones . . . but one stood alone as our favorite. When Curt found it, he said nothing at first, then moments later he whispered quietly, "Wow, Dad, that's good!" It was a picture of a misty morning on a calm lake. In a little skiff were a father and his son looking at the two corks floating at the ends of their fishing lines. The sun was tipping its hat over the mountains in the distance. Stretching across the scene was peace, refreshment, easygoing small talk. Two wistful words beneath the border appropriately released the message:

TAKE TIME.

In my younger years I was irritated with the well-worn tune attached to the old-fashioned sounding words of William Longstaff:

> *Take time to be holy,*
> *Speak oft with thy Lord;*
> . . . .
>
> *Take time to be holy,*
> *The world rushes on. . . .*

Twenty-five years, four children, many miles and mistakes later, those words make a lot of sense. They are like the psalmist's plea in Psalm 46:10:

CEASE STRIVING AND KNOW THAT I AM GOD. . . .
Or our Lord's counsel in Matthew 11:28:

COME TO ME . . . I WILL GIVE YOU REST.

Eight calm words from David. Eight restful words from Jesus. How unlike those eight panic words from the speedboat!

Listen . . . please listen! Is all your activity *that* important? Is it really necessary that you move *that* fast or that you drive at such breakneck speed? Why must you say yes to so many things that should be answered with a no? Could it be that your speed, your hurry-up lifestyle, is nothing more than a cheap narcotic to numb the pain of an empty life? Does *insecurity* require of you such intense acceleration? Is it *guilt* that drives your boat at full throttle? Maybe it's just a habit you've fallen into of choking down your food, talking too much and too fast (often without thought), and simply planning too many things in your schedule. All of this communicates volumes as you ricochet through your day. People get the definite impression that the only way to get next to you is to get in, sit down, shut up, and hang on.

An incredible observation regarding Jesus Christ came to my attention some time back. Not once does the Bible report that He *rushed* anywhere. He was often busy, but never in a mad dash. And yet He perfectly accomplished all the Father designed for Him to do. When you stop to think it over, His greatest accomplishment occurred the day He silenced the message of the snake.

It's About Time

I'm a sucker for time-management books.

Some people can't say no to a salesman at the door. Others have the hardest time passing up a free puppy . . . or driving by a garage sale without stopping. Still others find it almost impossible to withstand the urge to gamble. Not I. My weakness is books on the investment of my time—telling me how to replace being busy with being effective. Thinking through things before plunging into them. I often recall what Bernard Baruch once said:

> *Whatever failures I have known, whatever errors I have committed, whatever follies I have witnessed in private and public life, have been the consequences of action without thought.*

The antidote to that problem is described best by Paul in Ephesians 5:15-17:

> *Look carefully then how you walk! Live purposefully and worthily and accurately, not as the unwise and witless, but as wise—sensible, intelligent people; Making the very most of the time—buying up each opportunity—because the days are evil.*
> *Therefore do not be vague and thoughtless and foolish, but understanding and firmly grasping what the will of the Lord is* (The Amplified Bible).

It's verses like those that always grab my attention. Again I admit, there's this little alarm down inside my system that goes off whenever I sense that what I'm doing is a waste of energy, that there's a leak in my time dike I failed to plug. Without wanting to be neurotic about it, I get a little nervous when I think I am *not* living "purposefully," when I am failing to "buy up each opportunity," as Scripture so clearly commands. The verse that appears just before the passage I quoted shoves a long, pointed index finger into the chest of its reader as it shouts:

> *"Awake, O sleeper. . . ."*

Today, we'd say it like this: "Hey, wake up. Get with it, man!" The easiest thing in the world is to drift through life in a vague, thoughtless manner. God says there's a better way. He tells us to take time by the throat, give it a good shake, and declare: "That's it! I'm gonna manage you—no longer will you manage me!"

That's a major secret to living above our circumstances rather than under them. Let me mention a few specifics. Some people are always running late. Yes, always. *Punctuality* is simply a time-management matter. Some folks feverishly work right up to the deadline on every assignment or project they undertake. The job usually gets done . . . but the hassle, anxiety, and last-minute panic steal the fun out of the whole thing. *Starting early* and *pacing oneself* are time-management techniques. And some seem forever in a hurry, pushing and driving, occasionally *running* here and there. Again, another evidence of *poor planning*. Time management allows room for ease and humor, much-needed oil to soothe the friction created by motion.

Which brings us back to the counsel in Ephesians 5. Living purposefully, worthily, accurately . . . being sensible, intelligent, and wise in the rationing of our time.

In a book I just finished, *The Time Trap* (I told you I was a sucker for such volumes), I came upon a list of the most popular time wasters. They helped pinpoint some specific areas of frustration I must continually watch.

• Attempting too much at once
• Unrealistic time estimates
• Procrastinating
• Lack of specific priorities
• Failure to listen well
• Doing it myself—failure to delegate
• Unable to say no
• Perfectionism—focusing on needless details
• Lack of organization
• Failure to write it down
• Reluctance to get started
• Absence of self-appointed deadlines
• Doing first things first

Who hasn't heard the true story of Charles Schwab and Ivy Lee? Schwab was president of Bethlehem Steel. Lee, a consultant, was given the usual challenge: "Show me a way to get more things done with my time." Schwab agreed to pay him "anything within reason" if Lee's suggestion worked. Lee later handed the executive a sheet of paper with the plan:

> *Write down the most important tasks you have to do tomorrow. Number them in order of importance. When you arrive in the morning, begin at once on No. 1 and stay on it until it is completed. Recheck your priorities, then begin with No. 2 . . . then No. 3. Make this a habit every working day. Pass it on to those under you. Try it as long as you like, then send me your check for what you think it's worth.*

That one idea turned Bethlehem Steel Corporation into the biggest independent steel producer in the world within five years.

How much did Schwab pay his consultant? Several weeks after receiving the note, he sent Lee a check for $25,000, admitting it was the most profitable lesson he had ever learned.

Try it for yourself. If it works, great. But don't send me any money for the idea. I'd just blow it on another time-management book . . . which I don't have time to read.

Staying Alert

Your mind is a muscle. It needs to be stretched to stay sharp. It needs to be prodded and pushed to perform. Let it get idle and lazy on you, and that muscle will become a pitiful mass of flab in an incredibly brief period of time.

How can you stretch your mind? What are some good mental exercises that will keep the cobwebs swept away? I offer three suggestions:

READ. You may be too crippled and too poor to travel—but between the covers of a book are ideas and insights that await the joy of discovery. William Tyndale was up in years when he was imprisoned. Shortly before his martyrdom he wrote to the governor asking for:

> . . . a warmer cap, a candle, a piece of cloth to patch my leggings. . . . But above all, I beseech and entreat your clemency to . . . permit me to have my Hebrew Bible, Hebrew Grammar, and Hebrew Dictionary, that I may spend time . . . in study. [16]

The powers of your perception will be magnified through reading. Read wisely. Read widely. Read slowly. Scan. Read history as well as current events . . . magazines and periodicals as well as classics and poetry . . . biographies and novels as well as the daily news and devotionals.

Don't have much time? Neither did John Wesley. But his passion for reading was so severe he made it a part of his schedule—he read mostly *on horseback*. He rode between 50 and 90 miles a day with a book propped up on his saddle . . . and got through *thousands* of volumes during his lifetime. Knowing that reading attacks thickness of thought, Wesley told many a younger minister either to read—or get out of the ministry.

TALK. Conversation adds the oil needed to keep our mental machinery running smoothly. The give-and-take involved in rap sessions, the question-answer dialogue connected to discussion, provides the grinding wheel needed to keep us keen.

Far too much of our talk is surface jargon . . . shallow, predictable, obvious, pointless. Talk is too valuable to waste. Leave the discussion of people and weather to the newscasters! Delve into issues, ideas, controversial subjects, things that really matter. Ask and answer "why" and "how" . . . rather than "what" and "when." Probe. Question. Socrates was considered wise—not because he knew all the answers, but because he knew how to ask the right questions. Few experiences are more stimulating than eyeball-to-eyeball, soul-to-soul talks that force us to *think* and *reason* through specifics. For the sheer excitement of learning, talk!

WRITE. Thoughts disentangle themselves over the lips . . . and through the fingertips. How true! The old gray matter increases its creases when you put it down on paper. Start a journal. A journal isn't a diary. It's more. A journal doesn't record what you do—it records what you *think*. It spells out your ideas, your feelings, your struggles, your discoveries, your dreams. In short, it helps you articulate *who you are*.

Who knows? Your memoirs might make the bestseller list in the year 2000. And speaking of that, why not try writing an article for your favorite magazine? Editors are on a constant safari for rare species like you.

Francis Bacon provides a perfect close to hang on these lines:

> *Reading maketh a full man;*
> *Speaking, a ready man;*
> *writing, an exact man.*[17]

Starting Over

Instant replays have become old hat. We now expect them in all televised sports. Whether it's a tennis pro's impressive backhand or an NBA center's slam dunk or a heavyweight boxer's smashing jab, we never have to worry about missing it the first time around. It'll be back again and again and probably *again*.

It occurred to me recently that I'd enjoy (for lack of a better title) *delayed* replays of some of the more significant times in my life. But these would be different from fixed frames on film. In "delayed replays" I'm fantasizing the possibility of going back and being given another chance to relive a particular experience that could have been handled differently. More wisely. With greater tact. In better taste. You know, all those "if-I-had-that-to-do-over-again" thoughts. What a second chance that would be!

Just think of all the things we'd refrain from saying that we blurted out the first time around. And consider the different attitudes we would have toward unexpected interruptions, unplanned babies, unrealistic expectations, unimportant details. I really think we would take a lot more things a lot less seriously, don't you?

Fun times form great memories . . . so let's hear it for fewer frowns and more smiles. Laughter lingers. It soaks into the walls of a home, coming back to encourage us many years later.

Bob Benson captures all this so well in his piece, "Laughter In The Walls."

> I pass a lot of houses on my way home—
> some pretty,
> some expensive,
> some inviting—
> but my heart always skips a beat
> when I turn down the road
> and see my house nestled against the hill.
> I guess I'm especially proud
> of the house and the way it looks because
> I drew the plans myself.
> It started out large enough for us—
> I even had a study—
> two teenaged boys now reside in there.
> And it had a guest room—
> my girl and nine dolls are permanent guests.
> It had a small room Peg
> had hoped would be her sewing room—
> two boys swinging on the dutch door
> have claimed this room as their own.
> So it really doesn't look right now
> as if I'm much of an architect.

But it will get larger again—
one by one they will go away
to work,
to college,
to service,
to their own houses,
and then there will be room—
a guest room,
a study,
and a sewing room
for just the two of us.
But it won't be empty—
every corner
every room
every nick
in the coffee table
will be crowded with memories.
Memories of picnics,
parties, Christmases,
bedside vigils, summers,
fires, winters, going barefoot,
leaving for vacation, cats
conversations, black eyes
graduations, first dates,
ball games, arguments
washing dishes, bicycles
dogs, boat rides
getting home from vacation
meals, rabbits and
a thousand other things
that fill the lives
of those who would raise five.
And Peg and I will sit
quietly by the fire
and listen to the
laughter in the walls. [18]

Yes, if we had the benefit of "delayed replays," we would gain a lot of perspective on life we often miss the first time around.

But, unfortunately, second times around don't happen. We cannot rerear our children. I cannot repastor my first church. Initial impressions cannot be remade. Cutting remarks cannot be resaid. Scars can't be completely removed. Tear stains on the delicate fabric of our emotions are, more often than not, permanent. Memories are fixed, not flexible.

"You mean God won't forgive?"

You know better than that.

"And people can't overlook my failures?"

Come on, now. That's not the issue at all. Most people I know are amazingly understanding. Our biggest task is forgiving *ourselves*.

The main message is clear: Think before you speak. Pause before you act.

Another chance? No chance. It's absolutely impossible to go back and start over. Today is tomorrow's yesterday . . . and "delayed replays" will never occur. Today is memory in the making, a deposit in the bank of time. Let's make it a good one!

In the now-or-later battle for priorities, it's clear where the secret lies. Let's take care of the biggies now—today. It's amazing how the incidentals will fade away when we focus fully on the essentials. And that's impossible unless we put the important ahead of the urgent.

Tell me, what will be yesterday's replays in the tomorrows of your life? The answer is not that complicated. They will be the things your "walls" are absorbing today.

...ABOUT BALANCE AND EXTREMES

Balance. Extremes.

The enemy of our souls is the expert of extremes. Christ our Lord is the bulwark of balance. **Balance:** that essential equilibrium, ability to keep a level head, perspective, practical wisdom. **Extremes:** going too far in one direction, overreacting, losing control, having tunnel vision, fanaticism.

How often we find ourselves strung out because we failed to stay in touch with the whole picture. Zealous to do what is right, we get carried away. And soon we find ourselves embracing a distortion totally unaware that we are, in fact, dangerously near heresy. And the saddest part of all is this: No one is immune. It happens to the godly just as easily as it does to the wicked.

Blindspots result from getting things out of focus. Thanks to intensity and sincerity, we gravitate to greater extremes when others attempt to bring us back into balance with a word of caution. A kind reproof. A tug of warning. Nobody who is healthy really **wants** to be on the lunatic fringe.

Perhaps the following pages will assist you in a few areas where balance is needed . . . yet ever so difficult to maintain.

Let's make up our minds to get back in balance. And **stay** there.

Leading and Following

Picking scabs off wounds is not one of my favorite pastimes. On the contrary, I am normally repulsed by that kind of thing. If healing is happening, leave well enough alone. Don't tamper with the cast on the fractured leg. Don't change the prescription if the headache is leaving. Don't keep harping on issues or conflicts that have been resolved. Let it be. If I really want to get beyond my grief, for example, I can't afford to keep visiting the grave after the funeral.

But some rules occasionally have to be broken. If the bone in the leg isn't mending correctly, it is necessary to reset the thing. Even the dead must be exhumed when essential evidence is connected with the corpse.

And so—for only a few moments—I invite you to return with me to a scene all of us would rather forget, a cult compound in the steamy jungle of Guyana . . . Jonestown. Just reading the name sends a chill up my back. Atrocities far more horrible and extensive than that have transpired in history, I realize. But few more pathetic! Madmen have thrown the switch leading to the extermination of thousands. Millions, in fact. But never in *my* lifetime do I recall victims volunteering to drink poison, to feed it to their own children, to lie down without a fight (in rows!) and to die face

down . . . "looking like full-grown rag dolls," as one eyewitness later reported.

Death, I can accept. But one this bizarre, this meticulously choreographed, this blindly followed, I can hardly imagine. All of us played follow-the-leader as kids. But even then when the guide in front was too daring or foolish, we'd step aside. There were definite limits. But here lived 910 people, mostly adults, some full-family units, over whom their leader had *limitless control*. They were loyal to such ultimate extremes, he was free to devise, promote, rehearse, and finally carry out a paranoid suicide pact in broad daylight with virtually no restraint. And when the whole truth was disclosed, we all learned that the man had gone beyond the bounds of propriety and trust in his personal life. Except for a few defectors, the dictator was willingly supported in spite of prejudice, mismanagement of money, brutality, sexual perversion, and open blasphemy.

No one ever defined that follow-no-matter-what syndrome better than our Lord in Matthew 15:14:

> *"Let them alone; they are blind guides of the blind. And if a blind man guides a blind man, both will fall into a pit."*

Now, let's not toss the baby out with the bath water. An inappropriate reaction to the People's Temple carnage would be to say all strong leaders are suspect . . . to clip the wings of every visionary. Remember now, Jesus warned us against *blind* guides, not *all* guides. God is still using strategic, trustworthy, dedicated people as leaders. Always has, always will. Many guides have 20-20 vision as they continue walking with God.

But how can you tell when "blindness" starts to set in? What are the symptoms to look for in strong, natural leaders that tell you trouble is brewing? When should you stop following lest you too become blind? After thinking about this for quite awhile, I am ready to suggest six blindspots you dare not overlook.

1. *Authoritarianism.* Take care when the leader begins repressing your freedom. When he or she becomes inflexible, dictatorial, tyrannical, and oppressive . . . stop following. Observe how the guide treats others. If there is the lack of a servant's heart, if a teachable spirit is absent, pride is in control.

2. *Exclusiveness.* You should watch out for the "we-alone-are-right" and the "us-four-and-no-more" attitudes. When what is being promoted starts making you clannish, closed, and cliquish, *beware!* This will reveal itself in an encouragement to break commitments with your mate, family members, and long-standing friends. Paranoia often accompanies this exclusiveness.

3. *Greed.* Moneygrubbing is another tell-tale sign. Espe-cially if funds wind up in the leader's pocket and then become "nobody's business." Pay close attention to the leader's financial philosophy. Remember 1 Peter 5:2. Dependable shepherds aren't motivated by "sordid gain."

4. *Sensuality.* Moral purity is a must if the leader claims God's hand is on his life. Compromises here lead to consequences too severe to overlook. Follow no guru, no matter how visionary or charismatic, who promotes and practices sexual looseness, who is too familiar with the opposite sex, who laughs at lust and flirts with infidelity.

5. *Unaccountability.* Leaders who refuse to be accountable to anyone forfeit the right to be trusted and followed. Beware of the secretive, irresponsible, untouchable "I am God's anointed" mentality. No matter how eloquent or how competent, no one can sufficiently maintain a leadership role without counsel and occasional confrontation.

6. *Rationalization.* When wrong is justified with a defensive spirit, when inappropriate actions are quickly glossed over, when scriptural truth is twisted to fit a sinful life style, when gray-black facts are whitewashed, stop your support. Look for a sensitive conscience—a quick willingness to admit wrong in the one you follow.

Following a leader who is reliable and maintains your trust is both challenging and rewarding. But existing under the hypnotic, demanding spell of a blind prima donna is exactly as Christ described it: *the pits.*

Take His advice—"Let them alone!"

Adversity and Prosperity

There are two extreme tests that disturb our balance in life. Each has its own set of problems. On one side is *adversity*. Solomon realized this when he wrote:

> *If you faint in the day of adversity, your strength is small* (Proverbs 24:10, RSV).

The *Good News Bible* paraphrases that verse:

> *If you are weak in a crisis, you are weak indeed.*

Adversity is a good test of our resiliency, our ability to cope, to stand back up, to recover from misfortune. Adversity is a painful pedagogue.

On the other side is *prosperity*. In all honesty, it's a tougher test than adversity. The Scottish essayist and historian, Thomas Carlyle, agreed when he said:

> *Adversity is sometimes hard upon a man; but for one man who can stand prosperity, there are a hundred that will stand adversity.*[19]

Precious few are those who can live in the lap of luxury . . . who can keep their moral, spiritual, and financial equilibrium . . . while balancing on the elevated tightrope of success. It's ironic that most of us can handle a sudden demotion much better than a sizable promotion.

Why?

Well, it really isn't too difficult to explain. When adversity strikes, life becomes rather simple. Our need is to survive. But when prosperity occurs, life gets complicated. And our needs are numerous, often extremely complex. Invariably, our integrity is put to the test. And there is about one in a hundred who can dance to the tune of success without paying the piper named Compromise.

Now, before we get too carried away, let's understand that being successful isn't necessarily wrong. Being promoted, being elevated to a place of prominence can come from God Himself.

> *For not from the east, nor from the west,*
> *Nor from the desert comes exaltation;*
> *But God is the Judge;*
> *He puts down one, and exalts another* (Psalm 75:6-7).

Asaph, the guy who wrote those words, was correct. It is the Lord's sovereign right to demote as well as to promote . . . and we seldom know why He chooses whom.

Any biblical proof that some have been snatched from obscurity and exalted to prosperity without losing their integrity? Any examples of prosperous people who kept their balance while walking on the wire? Sure, several of them.

- Daniel was lifted from a lowly peon in a boot camp at Babylon to a national commander in charge of one-third of the kingdom (Daniel 6:1-2).
- Amos was promoted from a fig-picker in Tekoa, nothing more than an ancient sharecropper, to the prophet of God at Bethel, the royal residence of the king (Amos 7:14-15).
- Job was a rancher in Uz when God prospered him and granted him financial independence (Job 1:1-5).

And not one of the three lost his integrity in the process.

But the classic example is David, according to the last three verses of Psalm 78:

He also chose David His servant, And took him from the sheepfolds; From the care of the ewes with suckling lambs He brought him, To shepherd Jacob His people, And Israel His inheritance. So he shepherded them according to the integrity of his heart, And guided them with his skillful hands.

As Jehovah scanned the Judean landscape in search of Saul's successor, He found a youth in his mid-teens who possessed a unique combination:

the humility of a servant,

the heart of a shepherd,

the hands of skill.

And by his thirtieth birthday, Jesse's youngest held the premier office in his nation. King. At his fingertips was a vast treasury, unlimited privileges, and enormous power.

And how did he handle such prosperity? Read that final verse again. He shepherded the nation "according to integrity." He was Carlyle's "one in a hundred."

Are *you*?

If so, when you give your word, you do it. Exactly as you said you would. Because integrity means you are verbally trustworthy. Furthermore, when the bills come due, you pay them. Because integrity means you are financially dependable. Also, when you're tempted to mess around with an illicit sexual affair, you resist. Because integrity means you are morally pure. You don't fudge because you're able to cover your tracks. Neither do you fake it because you're now a big shot. Being successful doesn't give anybody the right to call wrong right. Or the okay to say something's okay if it isn't okay.

Adversity or prosperity, both are tough tests on our balance. To stay balanced through adversity, resiliency is required. But to stay balanced through prosperity—ah, that demands *integrity.* The swift wind of compromise is a lot more devastating than the sudden jolt of misfortune.

That's why walking on a wire is harder than standing up in a storm. Height has a strange way of disturbing our balance.

In Step and Out of Step

Staying in step with our times is basic.

Better than any other word I can think of, *change* describes our world. Vast, sweeping changes, especially in the last 150 years. The ability to shift with those changes—to maintain our precarious balance—is crucial. Simply to survive requires adjusting. To go further and make any kind of significant dent calls for an incredible amount of "flex," a quick willingness to alter the style and to modify methods. The old Roman politician, Publius, was right on when he wrote:

It is a bad plan that admits of no modification.[20]

And I don't mean just slightly. Some things must undergo drastic alterations if we hope to stay on the front edge of the wedge. Consider three of the more pronounced changes in our world.

POPULATION. It was not until 1850 that the number of people on this globe reached one billion. By 1930 (a mere eighty years later) the number doubled. Thirty years later —1960—it shot up to three billion. Since then the "fourth" billion human beings have come on the scene. And in only four more years from now, in 1985, earth will reach five billion. Demographers project that by the end of this century, another *two billion* will have been added . . . making seven billion bodies moving and eating and talking and struggling on this planet. The sheer press of people is staggering. No one can even think of maintaining an 1850 mentality in the swelling wave of such an enormous population growth. Ours is a completely different world than it was 131 years ago. *Profoundly* different.

SPEED. Until the early 1800's the fastest any human being could travel was about 20 miles per hour—on the back of a galloping horse. By 1880 the "streamline" passenger train whipped along at 100 miles per hour, an unheard of and fearsome velocity for mankind to experience. That was *nothing!* On December 17, 1903, at Kitty Hawk, North Carolina, a strange machine became airborne for 59 seconds as it zipped along for 852 feet. The Wrights' flight opened a whole new dimension of speed never dreamed possible. Less than 60 years later passenger jet planes swept along at 600+ miles per hour. If we were to include the ability of manned space rockets, the speed would jump to 16,000 miles per hour. Friends and neighbors, that's truckin' along!

BOOKS. If my research is correct, relatively few works were published until the end of the seventeenth century . . . and then only a few hundred in all the world. By the end of the nineteenth century, wow! About 25,000 books per year were being released. What about today? Well, hang on to your hat. No less than 400,000 new titles are now annually produced around our globe. Those are not all the books available, those are the *new* ones. Each year. And the number is increasing. And so is the literacy rate.

No need to keep stacking the facts in front of you, the point is obvious. And I haven't even bothered to mention technological advancements in the last century. Or the enormous changes made in military armament and defense . . . in agricultural processes, in housing, modes of transportation, medicine, music, architecture and engineering, films and entertainment, luxury items and personal conveniences, computers, clothing, and cars.

Since God is eternally relevant, since none of this blows Him away (omniscience can't be mind-boggled!), He is still in touch, in control, and fully aware. Why he has caused or allowed this radical reshaping of human history, nobody can say for sure. But we can reasonably surmise that God is up to something. Some would suddenly shout, "These are signs predicting Christ's soon return." Quite possibly. But what about until then? What is essential? We're back where we

started, aren't we? Being adaptable, willing to shift and change.

With changes come new challenges, things our fathers and grandfathers never faced. Take communication. The way it was done in the 1800s and early 1900s is "out of it" today. We must hammer out new and fresh styles on the anvil of each generation . . . always guarding against being dated and institutionalized. This calls for creativity, originality, and sensitivity. It also means being unwilling to fit into the horse-and-buggy mold of traditional expectations while living in a Concorde generation.

More than anything else, I'm convinced, the thing that attracted people to Jesus was His fresh, authentic, original style in a world of tired phrases, rigid rules, and empty religion. Remember the report made to the Pharisees? "Nobody ever spoke like this man." He marched to a fresh, new cadence.

Will it work? Is it worth the effort? Staying in step with our times is not without its perils—remember, they crucified Christ—there's something a whole lot more painful in the long march. And that's being out of step with today's drumbeat.

Shouting louder and stomping won't change the cadence, you know.

Public and Private

Balance between public life and private life is so important. And often misunderstood.

There are times my heart really goes out to our President. Not only does he have the toughest job in the world, in addition to that he cannot win, no matter what he decides. Since doves and hawks will never coexist, there is no way he'll ever get them in the same cage together. There must be times when he begins to doubt his own value . . . times when he fears the footsteps of his critics and wonders if they may be right. That Oval Office has to be the loneliest place in America. The only comfort the man has is that *he is not unique.* Every President who preceded him experienced similar struggles. Being the Chief includes that occupational hazard.

I was reminded of this recently when I read of a television program concerned with that most staid of subjects—a library. This, however, was the Library of Congress, and the BBS's former chairman, Sir Huw Wheldon, was standing in a forest of card index files. The program had all the makings of a slow-moving, dull documentary until. . . .

About halfway through, Dr. Daniel Boorstin, our Librarian of Congress, brought out a little blue box from a small closet that once held the library's rarities. The label on the box read: CONTENTS OF THE PRESIDENT'S POCKETS ON THE NIGHT OF APRIL 14, 1865.

Since that was the fateful night Abraham Lincoln was assassinated, every viewer's attention was seized.

Boorstin then proceeded to remove the items in the small container and display them on camera. There were five things in the box:

• A handkerchief, embroidered "A. Lincoln"
• A country boy's pen knife
• A spectacles case repaired with string
• A purse containing a $5 bill—*Confederate money (!)*
• Some old and worn newspaper clippings

"The clippings," said Boorstin, "were concerned with the great deeds of Abraham Lincoln. And one of them actually reports a speech by John Bright which says that Abraham Lincoln is one of the greatest men of all times."

Today, that's common knowledge. The world now knows that British statesman John Bright was right in his assessment of Lincoln, but in 1865 millions shared quite a contrary opinion. The President's critics were fierce and many. His was a lonely agony that reflected the suffering and turmoil of his country ripped to shreds by hatred and a cruel, costly war.

There is something touchingly pathetic in the mental picture of this great leader seeking solace and self-assurance from the comfort of a few old newspaper clippings as he reads them under the flickering flame of a candle all alone in the Oval Office.

Remember this: Loneliness stalks where the buck stops.

In the final analysis, top leaders pay a high price for their position. Think of some examples. Moses had no close chums. Nor did Joshua. You find David with Jonathan only in his earlier years—but when he became the monarch of Israel, his greatest battles, his deepest prayers, his hardest decisions occurred in solitude. The same with Daniel. And the other prophets? Loneliest men in the Old Testament. Paul frequently wrote of this in his letters. He informed his understudy, Timothy:

> . . . *all who are in Asia turned away from me* (2 Timothy 1:15).

Ever thought about Evangelist Billy Graham's life *apart from* his crusades and periodic public appearances? Or Corrie ten Boom? Or the president of a Christian institution? Do that for a moment or two. They would qualify as illustrations of A. W. Tozer's statement:

Most of the world's great souls have been lonely.[21]

Now don't misread this. It's not that the leader is aloof and unaccountable or purposely withdrawing or has something to hide—it's just the nature of the role. It is in lonely solitude that God delivers His best thoughts, and the mind needs to be still and quiet to receive them. And much of the weight of the office simply cannot be borne by others. Nor can those deep moments of meditation be shared in a busy seminar-like setting. Mystical though it may sound, it is absolutely essential that those whom God appoints to places of leadership learn to breathe comfortably in the thin air of the Himalayan heights where God's comfort and assurance come in the crushing silence of solitude. Where man's opinion is overshadowed. Where faith replaces fear. Where (as F. B. Meyer once put it) vision clears as the silt drops from the current of our life.[22]

It is there, alone and apart, true leaders earn the right to be respected. And learn the full meaning of those profound words, "Be still and know that I am God."

Expecting Perfection and Accepting Humanity

Not being a bumper-sticker freak, I find myself turned off by most of the stuff people announce on rear windows and back bumpers. With subjects like Iran in the news, I've had to do a lot of explaining to my younger kids . . . and sometimes they have had to help *me* out! Much of the junk is just plain repulsive—even some of the religious jargon.

But a couple of years ago I noticed a new one. For some reason it stuck in my cranium as firmly as on chrome. You've seen it dozens of times.

CHRISTIANS ARE NOT PERFECT, JUST FORGIVEN.

The last time I saw it was on the freeway on the back of the car that passed me while I was doing about 65. It fit. The time before that, I saw it on a VW bug (God love him) that had a ticket under the wiper because the meter was red. I tried to imagine the cop who checked the license number and saw the sticker. He was probably surprised Christians overpark!

Now before I emote all over this page, I need to set the record straight. There is no way we are *ever* going to convince all those outside the family of God that this is true. A few unbelievers understand, but most will *never* get that wired correctly. Instead, they will continue until their dying day being shocked and angered and offended and blown away whenever a Christian shows cracks in his or her life. Of all the things they can't seem to grasp, these two issues confuse them the most: God's grace and human depravity.

• How can something as marvelous as forgiveness of sins and eternal salvation be *free*?

• How can *that* person claim to be a Christian and act like that?

If you've done much witnessing, you know how often those two questions are asked. Non-Christians are stumped when it comes to the grace of God and the humanity of Christians. Why? Because their whole perspective is horizontal. Things that are valuable are costly. Therefore, it is inconceivable that something as priceless as heaven could be offered as a free gift. There isn't much grace running loose on the horizontal plane. And since their whole frame of reference is so man-centered, it's virtually impossible for them to imagine an individual who claims he belongs to God as one who still struggles with imperfection. After all, if you say God has come into your life and Christ has wiped your slate clean, how come you aren't perfect?

That's the non-Christian's way of thinking, and I accept that. They equate salvation with perfection—no wonder they're confused! But the Christian? Hey, we know better . . . or we certainly *should*. Being fellow members of one another, we understand that becoming a Christian in no way ushers us into a life of perfection, erasing our humanity and eradicating our depravity. If all that actually happened, then why in the world is the New Testament filled with counsel on forgiving others, understanding their failures, accepting their cracks, and focusing on their strengths (few though they may be)? It's one thing for an unbeliever to expect perfection—I can live with that and tolerate it fairly well—but it's *most* disconcerting to be pushed into a perfection mold by brothers and sisters who know better than that!

Oh, I understand that our example is Christ . . . and that our standard is high . . . and that our motives are often good. But it needs to be said again and again and again and again, CHRISTIANS ARE NOT PERFECT, JUST FORGIVEN.

How very easy it is to manipulate and even victimize our brothers and sisters! How quickly the thin thread of freedom snaps as heavyweights of perfectionistic expectations are placed upon us! Christ Jesus never did that with His own. When people were near Him there was this incredible magnetism because of an absence of unrealistic expectations and subtle demands and manipulative devices. He did not use pressure tactics. He simply accepted people as they were.

A paralysis sets in when we operate in the choking context of the perfection-expectation syndrome. Fed by fear and guilt, the Christian becomes a victim of others rather than a victor in Christ. You see, we ultimately act out those pressures and thereby limit our potential.

In one of Wayne Dyer's recent works—a bestseller for six months—he talks about how outside forces can limit our ability to achieve.

> *In the 1960s a teacher was given a roster showing the actual I.Q. test scores of the students of one class, and for another class a roster in which the I.Q. column had been [mistakenly] filled in with the students' locker numbers. The teacher assumed that the locker numbers were the actual I.Q.'s of the students when the rosters were posted at the beginning of the semester. After a year it was discovered that in the first class the students with high actual I.Q. scores had performed better than those with low ones. But in the second class the students with higher locker numbers scored significantly higher than those with lower locker numbers!*[23]

Believe me, if locker numbers can do it, so can the guilt brought on by Christians expecting perfection from one another. Let's back off! Let's relax the stranglehold on each others' necks. Let's allow the Lord to do the criticizing and finger-pointing and the demanding and the judging. Let's grow up and stop being so fragile and nit-picking. I love what Ruth Graham once so wisely said:

> *"It's my job to love Billy. It's God's job to make him good."*

Replace the name *Billy* with the name of your mate, your parent, your friend, your boss, your neighbor, your missionary, and especially your pastor, and you'll begin to get the drift of the bumper sticker's message. What's more, you'll be a lot easier to be around.

Remember, we've got to live with you, too.

Externals and Internals

Howard Snyder ticks me off.

He also makes me think. I agree, and I disagree. I laugh, and I sigh. Part of me wants to slug him yet two minutes later embrace him. I shake my head at his extreme generalizations . . . and shortly thereafter nod in amazement at his acute evaluations, accurate to the nth degree.

No man deserves all those emotions! But Snyder yanks them out of me as I read (for the third time) his 1976 controversial volume, *The Problem of Wine Skins.* Tough book. And don't let the title throw you. It has little to do with literal wine and even *less* with leather wineskins. But it has a lot to do with the principles behind Jesus' words in Luke 5:37-38.

> *No one puts new wine into old wineskins, for the new wine bursts the old skins, ruining the skins and spilling the wine. New wine must be put into new wineskins* (TLB).

Let that soak in. Obviously our Lord is distinguishing here between things that are essential (the wine) and things that are useful but not primary (the skins). Who needs wineskins if there is no wine? Wine, you see, represents the basics, the changeless, timeless, everpotent, always-necessary message. The gospel. The Savior. The pristine truth of Scripture.

And the wineskins? Clearly, they represent that which is secondary, subsidiary, man-made. Stuff like structure, traditions (now don't stop reading), and patterns of doing things which have grown up around and encased the "wine." Got the picture?

The wineskins are the point of contact between the wine and the world. And as the surrounding pressure mounts from society, the skins tend to cease being flexible. They are seldom replaced. They get thicker, hard, less elastic . . . and are ultimately unable to contain that volatile, vigorous vino within. They have reached the extreme of inflexibility. And, unfortunately, few indeed are those who can tolerate fresh, new, supple bags to contain the wine. We much prefer the old —even if it's brittle and leaks—rather than the new.

That was the rub in Jesus' day. He was too radical and fresh in His approach. He irritated the old guard. Frowning, they kept asking questions like:

> *"Why do Your disciples transgress the tradition of the elders? For they do not wash their hands when they eat bread"* (Matthew 15:2).

> *"Why do you eat and drink with the tax-gatherers and sinners?"* (Luke 5:30).

"Why are they (the disciples) *doing what is not lawful on the Sabbath?"* (Mark 2:24).

I mean, "Shame on you, Jesus! If you're going to expect our respect, keep your hands off the wineskins!"

You see, they confused the external container with the internal treasure—even though the old Judaistic hand-me-downs were leaking badly.

Today we applaud His revolutionary determination. It was *that* quality which caused His contemporaries to mumble, "No man ever spoke as this Man does." But the barriers He scaled and the accusations He received increased the level of public anger to intense proportions. He wound up nailed to a cross, remember. And many returned to their old wineskins of religious tradition, thinking they were now safe from His words that had worried them for over three years.

But a remnant had tasted the wine. They had cultivated a new appetite. With new hearts they sang new songs. They preached a new hope from the new covenant. As new creations in Christ they offered "a new and living way" (Hebrews 10:20). Emerging from a cocoon of fear and intimidation, they flew free and bold. Willing to live in dens and caves of the earth, they swept the old world off its feet . . . "they turned it upside down," they literally "upset the world" (Acts 17:6).

That new breed of nontraditional thinkers emerged again in the sixteenth century. Unwilling to be crushed in the iron jaws of the papacy and all its trappings, they broke loose. Why? They despised traditional wineskins. They refused to clothe the resplendent riches of Christ in tacky religious rags. They chose to preserve the wine and replace the skins at the cost of being misunderstood. In their day they were quickly branded "heretics." Yet—strangely—today we extol them as courageous "reformers." It's amazing what a few hundred years will do to our perspective.

And what about *you*? Busy protecting and trying to preserve the wineskins? Working overtime carrying a torch of external tradition? Hey, I understand. I did that for almost twenty years of my Christian life. The wine got little of my attention as I patched up wineskins year after year. *What a waste!* Through a process of time and very painful events, I am breaking that nervous habit. The older I get, the less I care about the traditional skins and the more I crave the pure wine, the essentials, the external internals.

Thanks, Howard Snyder. I needed the reminder. But you still tick me off!

Isolation and Involvement

Elevators are weird places, aren't they? Especially crowded ones.

You're crammed in close with folks you've never met, so you try really hard not to touch them. And nobody talks, either. The one thing you may hear is an occasional "Out, please" or "Oh, I'm sorry" as somebody clumsily steps on someone's toe. You don't look at anyone; in fact, you don't look anywhere but up, watching those dumb numbers go on and off. Strange. People who are all about the same height and speak the same language are suddenly as silent as a roomful of nuns when they occupy common space.

It's almost as if there's an official sign that reads:

NO TALKING, NO SMILING, NO TOUCHING, AND NO EYE CONTACT ALLOWED WITHOUT WRITTEN CONSENT OF THE MANAGEMENT. NO EXCEPTIONS!!

Years ago I was speaking on the campus of the University of Oklahoma. After the meeting, a crazy group of three or four guys invited me to have a Coke with them. Since we were several floors up in the student center, we decided to take the elevator down. As the door slid open, the thing was full of people who gave us that hey-you-guys-aren't-gonna-try-to-get-in-are-you? look. But we did, naturally. I was last. There wasn't even room to turn around. I felt the door close against my back as everyone stared in my direction. I smiled big and said loudly, "You might have wondered why we called this meeting today!" The place broke open with laughter. It was the most amazing thing to watch . . . people actually *talking*, actually *relating* to each other . . . *on an elevator.*

I've been thinking lately that an elevator is a microcosm of our world today: a large, impersonal institution where anonymity, isolation, and independence are the uniform of the day. A basic quality of our healthy social lives is being diluted, distorted, and demeaned by the "elevator mentality." We are way out of balance in the area of relating to people.

A recently published report by Ralph Larkin, a sociologist, on the crises facing suburban youth underscores several aspects of this new malaise of the spirit. Many children of American affluence are depicted as passively accepting a way of life they view as empty and meaningless. A syndrome is now set in motion that includes "a low threshold of boredom, a constricted expression of emotions, and an apparent absence of joy in anything that is not immediately consumable."[24] Makes sense when you observe the significant role now played by music, drugs, booze, sex, and status-symbol possessions. Take away rock concerts and sports events and you seldom witness much display of strong emotion.

Exit: Involvement and motivation. Enter: Indifference, noncommitment, disengagement, no sharing or caring . . . meals eaten with hi-fi headsets turned up loud, even separate bedrooms, each with a personal telephone, TV, and turntable, private toilet, and an it's-none-of-your-business attitude. No hassle . . . no conflicts . . . no accountability. No need to share. Or reach out. Or give a rip. Just watch the numbers and look at nobody.

Dr. Philip Zimbardo, a professor of psychology at Stanford and author of one of the most widely used textbooks in the field, addresses this issue in a *Psychology Today* article entitled "The Age of Indifference." He pulls no punches as he writes:

> *I know of no more potent killer than isolation. There is no more destructive influence on physical and mental health than the isolation of you from me and of us from them. It has been shown to be a central agent in the etiology of depression, paranoia, schizophrenia, rape, suicide, mass murder. . . .*

And then he adds:

> *The devil's strategy for our times is to trivialize human existence in a number of ways: by isolating us from one another while creating the delusion that the reasons are time pressures, work demands, or anxieties created by economic uncertainty; by fostering narcissism and the fierce competition to be No. 1. . . .*[25]

Ouch!

We must come to terms with all this. We must come down hard on it . . . the need is *urgent!* Our Savior modeled the answer perfectly. He didn't just preach it. He cared. He listened. He served. He reached out. He supported. He affirmed and encouraged. He stayed in touch. He walked with people . . . never took the elevator.

The only escape from indifference is to think of people as our most cherished resource. We need to work hard at re-establishing family fun, meaningful mealtimes, people involvement, evenings *without* the television blaring, nonsuperficial conversations, times when we genuinely get involved with folks in need—not *just* pray for them.

Stop the elevator. I want to get off.

...ABOUT LIFE AND DEATH

Life. Death.

Sweeping, broad terms. Too big to fully grasp. Yet basic, one-syllable words that encompass everything. **Life:** *birth, experiences, relationships, time, activities and involvements, choices and chances.* **Death:** *the finale, ultimate wrap-up, absolute silence and stillness, "the king of terrors," termination.*

How easy, how terribly tempting it is to cop out and refuse to come to terms with such profound stuff . . . to turn the TV up louder and lie back with a no-hassle, couldn't-care-less mentality. When it gets heavy, just switch to another channel.

But wait. There's reality to cope with. Life is short and uniquely designed for each one of us. And death is sure. It overlooks nobody. Strangely, although opposites, they work together, not unlike the sun and the moon—each impacting earth with its essential message.

And we are caught in between the currents. Forced to wrestle with life's questions and inequities. Expected to reach some conclusions during our threescore and ten. And then? You guessed it. Then it's curtains . . . then it's eternity. The big shift from the familiar to the incomprehensible. Awesome thought.

What's life about? What's beyond death? Are the answers for one related to the answers for the other?

You decide.

Is Trauma Terminal?

The definition reflects devastation:

TRAUMA: AN INJURY (AS A WOUND) TO LIVING TISSUE CAUSED BY AN EXTRINSIC AGENT . . . A DISORDERED PSYCHIC OR BEHAVIORAL STATE RESULTING FROM MENTAL OR EMOTIONAL STRESS. . . .[26] © 1980 by G. & C. Merriam Co., Publishers of the Merriam-Webster Dictionaries.

Like potatoes in a pressure cooker, we century-twenty creatures understand the meaning of stress. A week doesn't pass without a few skirmishes with those "extrinsic agents" that beat upon our fragile frames. They may be as mild as making lunches for our kids before 7:30 in the morning (*mild?*) or as severe as a collision with another car . . . or another person. Makes no difference. The result is "trauma" —a two-bit word for nervous. You know, the bottom-line reason *Valium* remains the top seller. Our emotional wounds are often deep. They don't hemorrhage like a stabbing victim, but they are just as real, just as painful . . . sometimes more.

Remember the stress test carried on by Dr. Thomas Holmes and his colleagues mentioned earlier in this book? They concluded that an accumulation of two hundred or more "life change units" in any year may mean more disruption—more trauma—than an individual can stand. On their scale, death of a spouse equals one hundred units, divorce represents seventy-three units . . . and Christmas equals twelve units![27] That helps explain the idea behind "something snapping" inside certain people when the final straw falls on them. Our capacity for trauma has its limits.

Joseph Bayly could certainly understand. He and his wife lost three of their children—one at eighteen days (after surgery); another at five years (leukemia); a third at eighteen years (sledding accident plus hemophilia). In my wildest imagination, I cannot fathom the depth of their loss. In the backwash of such deep trauma, the Bayly couple stood sometimes strong, sometimes weak, as they watched God place a period *before* the end of the sentence on three of their children's lives. And their anguish was not relieved when well-meaning people offered shallow, simple answers amidst their grief.[28]

H. L. Mencken must have had those situations in mind when he wrote:

There's always an easy solution to every human problem—neat, plausible, and wrong.[29]

Eyes that read these words might very well be near tears. You are trying to cope without hope. You are stretched dangerously close to the "200-unit" limit . . . and there's no relief on the horizon. You're bleeding and you've run out of bandages. You have moved from mild tension to advanced trauma.

Be careful! You are in the danger zone, emotionally. You're a sitting duck and the adversary is taking aim with both barrels loaded, hoping to open fire while you are vulnerable. Bam, *"Run!"* Boom! *"Think suicide."*

Listen carefully! Jesus Christ opens the gate, gently looks at you, and says:

> *Come to Me, all you who labor and are . . . over burdened, and I will cause you to rest—I will ease and relieve and refresh your souls* (Matthew 11:28, Amplified Bible).

Nothing complicated. No big fanfare, no trip to Mecca, no hypnotic trance, no fee, no special password. Just *come.* Meaning? Unload. Unhook the pack and drop it in His lap . . . now. Allow Him to take your stress as you take His rest. Does He know what trauma is all about? Remember, He's the One whose sweat became like drops of blood in the agony of Gethsemane. If anybody understands trauma, He does. Completely.

He's a master at turning devastation into restoration. His provision is profound, attainable, and right.

It's really a life-and-death issue.

Finishing the Course

Not enough is said or written today about *finishing* well.

Lots and lots of material is available on motivation to get started and creative ways to spark initiative. Plenty of advice is floating around on setting goals and establishing priorities and developing a game plan. All of it is insightful and needed. Getting off the dime is often a herculean task. Starting well is Plan "A," no doubt about it.

But let's hear it for the opposite end, for a change. Let's extol the virtues of sticking with something until it's *done.* Of hanging tough when the excitement and fun fade into discipline and guts. You know, being just as determined eight minutes into the fourth quarter as at the kickoff. Not losing heart even though the project has lost its appeal. Eugene Peterson, sounding a lot like the late A. W. Tozer, in his fine book, *A Long Obedience in the Same Direction,* expresses the same concern with these insightful words:

> *Our attention spans have been conditioned by thirty-second commercials. Our sense of reality has been flattened by thirty-page abridgments.*
>
> *It is not difficult in such a world to get a person interested in the message of the gospel; it is terrifically difficult to sustain the interest. Millions of people in our culture make decisions for Christ, but there is a dreadful attrition rate. . . . In our kind of culture anything, even news about God, can be sold if it is packaged freshly; but when it loses its novelty, it goes on the garbage heap. There is a great market for religious experience in our world; there is little enthusiasm for the patient acquisition of virtue, little inclination to sign up for a long apprenticeship in what earlier generations of Christians called holiness.*[30]

I fear our generation has come dangerously near the "I'm-getting-tired-so-let's-just-quit" mentality. And not just in the spiritual realm. Dieting is a discipline, so we stay fat. Finishing school is a hassle, so we bail out. Cultivating a close relationship is painful, so we back off. Getting a book written is demanding, so we stop short. Working through conflicts in a marriage is a tiring struggle, so we walk away. Sticking with an occupation is tough, so we start looking elsewhere. This reminds me of something my sister recently passed along to me, entitled *Six Phases of a Project:*

- Enthusiasm
  - Disillusionment
    - Panic
      - Search for the guilty
        - Punishment of the innocent
          - Praise and honors for the nonparticipants.

By the time a project has run its crazy course, confusion has replaced accomplishment. Participants have changed to spectators. The "let's-just-quit" mentality is upon us.

Ignace Jan Paderewski, the famous composer-pianist, was scheduled to perform at a great concert hall in America. It was an evening to remember—black tuxedos and long evening dresses, a high-society extravaganza full bore. Present in the audience that evening was a mother with her fidgety nine-year-old son. Weary of waiting, he squirmed constantly in his seat. His mother was in hopes that her boy would be encouraged to practice the piano if he could just hear the immortal Paderewski at the keyboard. So—against his wishes—he had come.

As she turned to talk with friends, her son could stay seated no longer. He slipped away from her side, strangely drawn to the ebony concert grand Steinway and its leather tufted stool on the huge stage flooded with blinding lights. Without much notice from the sophisticated audience, the boy sat down at the stool, staring wide-eyed at the black and white keys. He placed his small, trembling fingers in the right location and began to play "Chop Sticks." The roar of the crowd was hushed as hundreds of frowning faces turned in his direction. Irritated and embarrassed, they began to shout:

"Get that boy away from there!"

"Who'd bring a kid that young in here?"

"Where's his mother?"

"Somebody stop him!"

Backstage, the master overheard the sounds out front and quickly put together in his mind what was happening. Hurriedly, he grabbed his coat and rushed toward the stage. Without one word of announcement he stooped over behind the boy, reached around both sides, and began to improvise a countermelody to harmonize with and enhance "Chop Sticks." As the two of them played together, Paderewski kept whispering in the boy's ear:

"Keep going. Don't quit, son. Keep on playing . . . don't stop . . . don't quit."

And so it is with us. We hammer away on our project, which seems about as significant as "Chop Sticks" in a con-

cert hall. And about the time we are ready to give it up, along comes the Master, who leans over and whispers:

"Now keep going; don't quit. Keep on . . . don't stop; don't quit,"

as He improvises on our behalf, providing just the right touch at just the right moment.

Do I write today to a few weary pilgrims? Is the road getting long and hope wearing a little thin? Or to a few parents who are beginning to wonder if it's worth it all—this exacting business of rearing children, which includes cleaning up daily messes and living with all that responsibility? Or to you who have a dream, but seeing it accomplished seems too long to wait? Listen to the Master's whispering:

"Let us not lose heart in doing good, for in due time we shall reap if we do not grow weary" (Galatians 6:9).

"Therefore . . . be steadfast, immovable . . . your toil is not in vain in the Lord" (1 Corinthians 15:58).

"Be of sober spirit, be on the alert. . . . And after you have suffered for a little while, the God of all grace . . . will Himself perfect, confirm, strengthen and establish you" (1 Peter 5:8, 10).

So many start the Christian life like a lightning flash—hot, fast, and dazzling. But how many people (aged 60 and over) can you name who are finishing the course with sustained enthusiasm and vigor? Oh, there are some, I realize, *but why so few?* What happens along the way that swells the ranks of quitters? I really wish I knew that answer. If I did, I'd shout warnings from the pulpit Sunday after Sunday. No, better than that, I'd stoop over and whisper them to every discouraged person I meet. Before it's too late.

Before he quits, and, instead of mastering the *Minuet* or *Concerto in A Minor*, settles for "Chop Sticks."

The Relevance of Violence

Like slender sticks of dynamite taped together with a short fuse, our times are really threatening. Maybe *volatile* is a better description. Anger is ready to lunge into physical violence at the slightest provocation. Makes no difference whether it's a bunch of California lettuce farmers arguing with a union or a mob of angry prison inmates or that loaded cannon in the Middle East, this entire globe seems to be brimming with hostility, awaiting a nudge on an international hair trigger leading to full-scale disaster.

It's not just a vast global problem, however. It's personal. It's in your neighborhood. Your school. Down where you work. Gals don't jog after dark unless they carry a can of mace. Only fools leave their cars unlocked. Home security systems are no longer considered a luxury for the rich. Not even teachers are safe in the classroom. In one edition of *Phi Delta Kappan,* an educational journal, a high school teacher named Margaret Campbell tells of being hit across the back of her head with a large piece of wood swung by a student filled with rage. The sordid account, vividly entitled "Testimony of a Battered Teacher," describes the premeditated attack before offering eight suggestions to other teachers who will surely be victims of such trauma in the future.[31]

But I must confess, the final straw of shock came when I read of the murder of John White in a quiet neighborhood in southwest Cleveland. The killer? A man hired by White's two kids. That's right. His 17-year-old son and 14-year-old daughter paid $60 to have their own dad slain. As the police pieced the story together, an unbelievable report emerged. The hit man was hired to sit in the living room with a .38-caliber revolver in his lap. As White walked through his front door after work, the killer fired once and missed. Shot again and hit him in the arm. As the victim ran into the kitchen to escape through the back door, a third shot hit him in the head. The daughter, by the way, waited in another room until the fatal shot was fired.

Then what? Well, the teenagers paid off the murderer with money from their dad's pocket then hid the body in a back room. After that they cashed his last paycheck and used his credit cards to go on a 10-day spending spree. They spent about $2,000 on televisions, video games, bicycles, and other amusements as well as food and various entertainment activities. While the body was decaying in the utility room, they were cooking meals in the kitchen a few feet away and enjoying themselves in the living room. "It was life as usual," said a Cleveland police investigator. After being caught, they openly confessed the entire, bizarre event. When asked why, they answered:

He wouldn't let us do anything we wanted, like smoke pot.

The dad had angered the kids by trying to enforce an evening curfew . . . and by not allowing them to quit school. So they had him knocked off. Perhaps I should add that the killer was a 19-year-old friend of the White children.

Slumped over a soiled piece of parchment under the eerie glow of candlelight in a stone dungeon, the aged Paul wrote his last few sentences. But they stab us awake with incredible relevance.

. . . realize this, that in the last days difficult times will come. For men will be . . . arrogant, revilers, disobedient to parents, ungrateful, unholy . . . brutal, haters of good, treacherous, reckless . . . (2 Timothy 3:1-4).

The Greek term he chose for "difficult times" means, literally, "fierce, harsh, hard to deal with, savage." It is used only one other time in all the New Testament as two demonized men are seen as "exceedingly violent" (Matthew 8:28). An apt description of our times. Exceedingly violent. Operation powder keg. Ready to explode.

There is a glimmer of hope amid this flood of violence. It is this: Christ's coming cannot be far away. These "last days" of pain—slowly though they may seem to pass—are daily reminders that our redemption draws near. And "we shall all be changed, in a moment, in the twinkling of an eye . . . (1 Corinthians 15:51, 52).

Like, fast. Really fast. Faster than a short fuse on sticks of dynamite.

A War Among Stars?

For the next few minutes, imagine this scene:

But the day of the Lord will come like a thief, in which the heavens will pass away with a roar and the elements will be destroyed with intense heat, and the earth and its works will be burned up. Since all these things are to be destroyed in this way, what sort of people ought you to be in holy conduct and godliness, looking for . . . the coming of the day of God, on account of which the heavens will be destroyed by burning, and the elements will melt with intense heat! (2 Peter 3:10-12)

Scary stuff, that business about the heavens passing away and the astronomical destruction and the twice-mentioned "intense heat" that will result in a total wipeout of planet earth. Makes me wonder *how*. Always has. I've heard the same things you have about superatomic warheads and hydrogen bombs in World War III. But somehow that never explained how "the heavens will pass away" or how the surrounding atmosphere and stratosphere could be "destroyed by burning."

Since that would usher in "the day of God," I've always had reservations that He would use men's fireworks to announce His arrival. If I read these verses correctly, they describe such phenomenal destructive force it would make our armory of demolition devices look like a two-bit firecracker under a tin can. It's impossible to imagine!

But in my reading recently I stumbled across a possible breakthrough. It may be a hint on how the Lord might be planning to pull off this final blast.

On March 9, 1979, nine satellites stationed at various points in the solar system simultaneously recorded a bizarre event deep in space. It was, in fact, *the most powerful burst of energy ever recorded*. Astronomers who studied the readings were in awe, mumbling to themselves.[32]

The burst of gamma radiation lasted for only one-tenth of a second . . . but in that instant it emitted as much energy as the sun does in 3000 years. An astrophysicist named Doyle Evans, who works at the Los Alamos Scientific Laboratories in New Mexico, said the energy being emitted was at a rate of 100 billion times greater than the energy emission rate of the sun. If the gamma ray burst had occurred in the Milky Way galaxy, it would have set our entire atmosphere aglow. If the sun had suddenly emitted the same amount of energy, our earth would have vaporized. Instantly.

There's more. The satellites were able to pinpoint the location of the burst to a spot in a galaxy known as N-49, which is associated with the remnants of a super nova believed to have exploded about ten thousand years ago. When a star explodes into a super nova, the outer shell is blown away and the inner core condenses from its own gravity to create a neutron star. That core becomes a single, huge nucleus, shrinking from a size larger than the sun (860,000 miles in diameter) to a compact ball no more than five miles across. Those neutrons are so incredibly dense that one cubic inch weighs 20 million, million pounds.

As untrained and ignorant as we may be of the technical side of all this, I suggest it might cast some light on the validity of Peter's remark. At least, in my estimation, it makes a lot more sense than atomic wars.

It's probably going to be more like star wars.

And I have no plans to be around at the premiere showing. How about you?

My Dad and His Death

My dad died last night.

He left like he had lived. Quietly. Graciously. With dignity. Without demands or harsh words or even a frown, he surrendered himself—a tired, frail, humble gentleman—into the waiting arms of his Savior. Death, selfish and cursed enemy of man, won another battle.

As I stroked the hair from his forehead and kissed him goodbye, a hundred boyhood memories played around in my head.

• When I learned to ride a bike, he was there.

• When I wrestled with the multiplication table, his quick wit erased the hassle.

• When I discovered the adventure of driving a car, he was near, encouraging me.

• When I got my first job (delivering newspapers), he informed me how to increase my subscriptions and win the prize. It worked!

• When I mentioned a young woman I had fallen in love with, he pulled me aside and talked straight about being responsible for her welfare and happiness.

• When I did a hitch in the Marine Corps, the discipline I had learned from him made the transition easier.

From him I learned to seine for shrimp. How to catch flounder and trout and red fish. How to open oyster shells and fix crab gumbo . . . and chili . . . and popcorn . . . and make rafts out of old inner tubes and gunny sacks. I was continually amazed at his ability to do things like tie fragile mantles on the old Coleman lantern, keep a fire going in the rain, play the harmonica with his hands behind his back, and keep three strong-willed kids from tearing the house down.

Last night I realized I had him to thank for my deep love for America. And for knowing how to tenderly care for my wife. And for laughing at impossibilities. And for some of the habits I have picked up, like approaching people with a positive spirit rather than a negative one, staying with a task until it is finished, taking good care of my personal belongings, keeping my shoes shined, speaking up rather than mumbling, respecting authority, and standing alone (if necessary) in support of my personal convictions rather than giving in to more popular opinions. For these things I am deeply indebted to the man who raised me.

Certain smells and sounds now instantly remind me of my dad. Oyster stew. The ocean breeze. Smoke from an expensive cigar. The nostalgic whine of a harmonica. A camping lantern and white gas. Car polish. Fun songs from the 30s and 40s. Freshly mowed grass. A shrill whistle from a father to his kids around supper time. And Old Spice aftershave.

Because a father impacts his family so permanently, I think I understand better than ever what the Scripture means when Paul wrote:

> *Having thus a fond affection for you, we were well-pleased to impart to you not only the gospel of God but also our own lives, because you had become very dear to us. . . . just as you know how we were exhorting and encouraging and imploring each one of you as a father would his own children, so that you may walk in a manner worthy of the God who calls you into His own kingdom and glory* (1 Thessalonians 2:8, 11-12).

Admittedly, much of my dad's instruction was indirect —by model rather than by explicit statement. I do not recall his overt declarations of love as clearly as I do his demonstrations of it. His life revolved around my mother, the darling and delight of his life. Of that I am sure. When she left over nine years ago, something of him died as well. And so—to her he has been joined and they are, together, with our Lord. In the closest possible companionship one can imagine.

In this my sister, my brother, and I find our greatest comfort—they are now forever *with the Lord*—eternally freed from pain and aging and death. Secure in Jesus Christ our Lord. Absent from the body and at home with Him. And with each other.

Last night I said goodbye. I'm still trying to believe it. You'd think it would be easy since his illness had persisted for more than three years. How well I remember the Sunday he suffered that first in a series of strokes as I was preaching. God granted him several more years to teach many of us to appreciate the things we tend to take for granted.

He leaves in his legacy a well-marked Bible I treasure, a series of feelings that I need to deepen my roots, and a thousand memories that comfort me as I replace denial with acceptance and praise.

I await heaven's gate opening in the not-too-distant future. So do other Christians, who anxiously await Christ's return. Most of them anticipate hearing the soft strum of a harp or the sharp, staccato blast of a trumpet.

Not me. I will hear the nostalgic whine of a harmonica . . . held in the hands of the man who died last night . . . *or did he?* The memories are as fresh as this morning's sunrise.

My Lord and His Return

The other evening my wife and I were enjoying a quiet conversation together. We were sipping some fresh-perked coffee, the house was unusually still, and there were no plans to go anywhere that evening. You know, one of those priceless moments you wish you could wrap up and reserve for later use when it's really needed again.

For some strange reason our discussion turned to the subject of Christ's return. Almost out of the blue, I found myself tracking that thought further than I have for months. Cynthia and I chuckled at some comments each one made about letting the folks in the tribulation worry with the hassles that we have to handle now—like cleaning out our garage or landscaping the backyard! We also smiled together contemplating the joys that will be ours to share our lives throughout eternity with family and friends in the Body of Christ.

As time passed the balance of that evening, I kept returning to the thought, "He *is* coming back. What a difference it will make!" It is remarkable, when you stop and get specific about it, how many things we take for granted will suddenly be removed or changed drastically. Think about that. . . .

Is it a waste to focus on the Lord's descent? Quite the contrary. It's biblical; it's the very thing Titus 2:13 says we ought to do:

> *Looking for the blessed hope and the appearing of the glory of our great God and Savior, Christ Jesus.*

When's the last time you—on your own—meditated on that fact? If you're like me it's been too long. People who are more practical than mystical, who are realistic rather than idealistic, tend to shove that stuff to times like funerals or near-death experiences. Most of us are here-and-now thinkers much more than then-and-there people. But Scripture says we are to "comfort one another" (1 Thessalonians 4:13-18) with information about Jesus' return for us. It says these truths form the very foundation of a "steadfast, immovable, always abounding" lifestyle (1 Corinthians 15:50-58). Listen, this Bible of ours is full and running over with promises and encouragements directly related to the return of our Lord Christ. I just checked, it's not just hinted at, it's *highlighted*, it's an obvious theme of New Testament truth. You can't read very far without stumbling upon it no matter which book you choose. In the New Testament alone the events related to Christ's coming are mentioned over three hundred times. It's like white on rice.

Critics have denied it. Cynics have laughed at it. Scholars have ignored it. Liberal theologians have explained it away (they call that "rethinking" it) and fanatics have perverted it. "Where is the promise of His coming?" (2 Peter 3:4) many still shout sarcastically. The return of our Savior will continue to be attacked and misused and denied. But there it stands, solid as a stone, soon to be fulfilled, ready to offer us hope and encouragement amidst despair and unbelief.

"Okay, swell. But what do I do in the meantime?" I can hear a dozen or more pragmatists asking that question. First, it might be best for you to understand what you *don't* do. You don't sit around, listening for some bugle call. You don't keep staring up into the sky, looking for the rapture cloud. You don't whip up a white robe and buy a helium-filled balloon with angels painted all over it. And you don't quit work and move to Oregon for fear you'll miss Him because of the smog. And for goodness sake, don't try to set the date because of the "signs of the times"!

You *do* get your act together. You *do* live every day (as if it's your last) for His glory. You *do* work diligently on your job and in your home (as if He isn't coming for another ten years) for His Name's sake. You *do* shake salt out every chance you get . . . and *do* shine the light . . . and remain balanced, cheerful, winsome, and stable, anticipating His return day by day. Other than that, I don't know what to tell you.

Except, maybe, if you're not absolutely sure you're ready to fly, you get your ticket *fast*. As long as they are available, they're free. But don't wait. About the time you finally make up your mind, the whole thing could have happened, leaving you looking back instead of up.

What good is a ticket if the event is over?

A DECISION . . .
BLACK AND WHITE

We've thought about a lot of issues in these pages. There are more—many more—but few more important than those having to do with truth and error, now and later, balance and extremes, life and death.

Unless you hurriedly skimmed through the book, you've probably wrestled with some of the things you read. That's good. In fact, that's essential. No way can anyone honestly make up his mind without a struggle. Tough, lasting decisions are like brand new babies; they are born through a painful process. And the more difficult the decision, the greater the pain.

Between the lines you may have noticed an underlying message. I chose to keep it subtle rather than repeatedly punch and pound away on you. Why? Because I respect you who read my words. The whole emphasis I've been trying to communicate has been your ability to think and reason and decide on the basis of faith in the facts . . . *not* feelings. You didn't need something else rammed down your throat while you were biting off and chewing up some rather sizable chunks of information page after page.

But neither my respect nor my style allows me the freedom to write the final period without directly addressing the sin- gle most important issue in all of life. I'm referring to your re- lationship with the living God . . . how you can know Him in a personal and meaningful way.

Nineteen centuries ago Jesus Christ died on behalf of the sins of mankind. Shortly afterward He was bodily raised from the dead—an astounding miracle. He still lives. His death and resurrection provided the way of access to God. But this doesn't mean that all people are in God's family. No. But it *does* mean that people like you and me are now able to *be* forgiven and fully accepted . . . if we simply believe that Jesus Christ died (and was raised from death) on our behalf —for us personally.

Now, of all things that you must decide on, none is more significant than this. And no one can do this for you or offer you an alternative plan that God will approve. You yourself must personally accept the gift of eternal life through faith in Jesus Christ. You alone must make up your mind regarding Christianity. You are important . . . a valuable, worthwhile, significant person with an eternal soul. God graciously reaches down to you today and extends his love and forgive- ness. He offers you eternal life.

Why? Let me repeat it: because He values your worth. You

are important to Him. Your response—even though it represents only one among billions of people on earth—is more significant than you can imagine.

Make up your mind today.

Footnotes

1. John R. W. Stott, *The Preacher's Portrait* (Grand Rapids: Wm. B. Eerdmans Publishing Company, 1961), p. 29.

2. John Bartlett, ed., *Familiar Quotations* (Boston: Little, Brown and Company, 1955), p. 599.

3. Walter Martin, *Screwtape Writes Again* (Santa Ana, California: Vision House Publishers, 1975), p. 16.

4. Leo Rangell, M.D., *The Mind of Watergate* (New York: W. W. Norton & Company, 1980), pp. 24-25.

5. Robert Kafahl and Kelly Segraves, *The Creation Explanation* (Wheaton: Harold Shaw Publishers, 1975), p. 151.

6. Leslie B. Flynn, *Man: Ruined and Restored* (Wheaton: Victor Books, 1978), pp. 9-10.

7. Marilee Zdenek, *Splinters in my pride*, Part 1 (Waco, Texas: Word Books, 1979), [n.p.].

8. T. H. Holmes and R. H. Rahe, "The Social Readjustment Rating Scale," *Journal of Psychosomatic Research* II (1967): 213-18. Copyright 1967 Pergamon Press, Ltd.

9. Frank B. Minirth, M.D., and Paul D. Meier, M.D., *Happiness is a Choice* (Grand Rapids: Baker Book House, 1978), p. 132.

10. Ronald M. Enroth, "The Power Abusers," *Eternity*, October 1979 (Philadelphia: Evangelical Ministries, Inc.), p. 25.

11. Peter F. Drucker, *The Effective Executive* (New York: Harper & Row Publishers, 1966), p. 143.

12. Cathy Trost and Ellen Grzech, "What Happened When 5 Families Stopped Watching TV," *Good Housekeeping* Magazine, August 1979, pp. 94, 97-99.

13. Urie Bronfenbrenn, "TV and Your Child," *Christian Medical Society Journal*, Haddon Robinson, ed. (Richardson, Texas: Christian Medical Society, 1978), p. 7.

14. Ibid., back cover.

15. Philip Yancey, *Where Is God When It Hurts?* (Grand Rapids: Zondervan Publishing House, 1977), pp. 91-92.

16. J. Oswald Sanders, *Spiritual Leadership* (Chicago: Moody Press, 1967), p. 94.

17. Ibid.

18. Bob Benson, the poem "Laughter in the Walls" is from the book *Laughter in the Walls* (Nashville: Impact Books, 1969), and is used by permission.

19. John Bartlett, p. 475.

20. Ibid., p. 44.

21. J. Oswald Sanders, p. 108.

22. F. B. Meyer, *Moses* (Grand Rapids: Zondervan Publishing House, 1953), p. 32.

23. Dr. Wayne W. Dyer, *Pulling Your Own Strings* (New York: Avon Books, 1978), p. 13.

24. Philip G. Zimbardo. "The Age of Indifference," *Psychology Today*, August 1980, p. 72.

25. Ibid., p. 72, 74.

26. *Webster's New Collegiate Dictionary* (Springfield, Massachusetts: G. & C. Merriam Company, 1980), p. 1234.

27. T. H. Holmes and R. H. Rahe, pp. 213-218.

28. Joseph Bayly, *The Last Thing We Talk About* (Elgin, Illinois: David C. Cook Publishing Co., 1973), p. 66.

29. H. L. Mencken, *The Vintage Mencken*, Alistair Cooke, ed., (New York: Vintage Books), 1955. Copyright by Alfred A. Knopf, Inc., 1955. pp. 240.

30. Eugene Peterson, *A Long Obedience in the Same Direction* (Downers Grove, Illinois: InterVarsity Press, 1980), pp. 11, 12.

31. Margaret H. Campbell, "Testimony of a Battered Teacher," *Phi Delta Kappan*, February 1979, p. 441.

32. Ronald Kotulak, "Astronomers Awestruck by Powerful Burst of Energy," *Dallas Times Herald*, 28 January 1980.